ROBERT LOWELL
The Old Glory

ROBERT LOWELL (1917–77) was the author of many books of poetry. He won the Pulitzer Prize for *Lord Weary's Castle* (1947) and *The Dolphin* (1974) and the National Book Award for *Life Studies* (1960). FSG published his *Collected Prose* in 1987.

Books by ROBERT LOWELL

Collected Prose (1987)

The Oresteia of Aeschylus (1978)

Day by Day (1977)

Selected Poems (1976)

The Dolphin (1973)

History (1973)

For Lizzie and Harriet (1973)

Notebook (1969)
(Revised and expanded edition, 1970)

Prometheus Bound (1969)

The Voyage and other versions of poems by Baudelaire (1969)

Near the Ocean (1967)

The Old Glory (1965)

For the Union Dead (1964)

Imitations (1961)

Phaedra (translation) (1961)

Life Studies (1959)

The Mills of the Kavanaughs (1951)

Lord Weary's Castle (1946)

Land of Unlikeness (1944)

The Old Glory

Robert Lowell

The Old Glory

Three Plays

Farrar, Straus and Giroux
New York

Farrar, Straus and Giroux
19 Union Square West, New York 10003

To Jonathan Miller
and Randall Jarrell

My sources have been Nathaniel Hawthorne's stories and sketches, *Endecott and the Red Cross*, *The Maypole at Merry Mount* and *My Kinsman, Major Molineux;* Thomas Morton's *New Canaan;* and Herman Melville's *Benito Cereno*.

R.L.

Note on the revised edition (1968)

Of the three plays in this trilogy, only *Endecott and the Red Cross* has been changed. It has been lengthened to give it substance, so that it might act by itself, or give supporting force to *Benito Cereno,* if on some Methuselah's evening all three plays were presented together. What I have added are mostly Indians. Innumerable lines have been "improved" to be stronger, to be quieter, less in character, more in character.

R.L.

Contents

ENDECOTT &
THE RED CROSS

Endecott and the Red Cross
in order of appearance

Assawamset

Thomas Morton

Mr. Blackstone

Edward

Edith

Sergeant

Soldier

Governor Endecott

Palfrey

Soldiers

Indians

Revellers: Maskers, dancers, people of Merry Mount

Darkened stage. Glow of red coals in the background. ASSA-
WAMSET, the chief of the Narraganset, a large kingly man, stands
facing THOMAS MORTON, the Master of Merry Mount. In the shadows,
dimly seen figures of Englishmen and Indians.

ASSAWAMSET

Death has brought me back to you.

MORTON

Death?

ASSAWAMSET

Seven days I fasted, and on the eighth
a voice said, "Go forward, turn
no more than the geese flying south."
Carrying only my bow and a roll of furs,
I marched south, turning no more than the geese.
Seven days, seven nights, and on the eighth
as I sat cooking my evening meal
on a meadow by a brook's edge,
I saw three clearings in the forest,
three well-beaten paths. They shone
and whistled like burning arrows.

MORTON

What then? Could you walk on those paths?

ASSAWAMSET

No, I entered the first path.
The forest was on fire.
I entered the second path.
Once again the forest was on fire.
Then I tried the third. This too was fire, but false fire . . .
I felt nothing,
and journeyed straight forward another day,
and came to a mountain, steep rock,
and white as ermine. And there on the top
you sat.

MORTON

I couldn't have been there,
I have been expecting you here, many days.
You are slow.

ASSAWAMSET

No, you were sitting on top of the mountain,
and loudly laughing at me. Your skin and robe
were as white as bleached bones. I saw
you were the servant of the Master of life,
but I didn't know how to reach you,
for there was no foothold in the rock.
Then you said, "Take off your clothes, Assawamset,
and bathe in the brook. Then break your bow,
and throw me all your furs." I obeyed.
When I had bathed and broken my bow,
and given you my furs, you threw me a gun.
"Fire into the rock," you said. And when

I fired, suddenly I saw I had blasted a stairway
in the rock, and when I climbed
to where you sat, the mountain had changed
to a great plain, and you were gone.
And then a voice was saying,
"I am the maker and unmaker of earth and sky,
the trees, the brooks, the mountains,
fish, bird, beast and man,
their breath that comes, their breath that goes.
Because I love you, I have sent Thomas Morton to you,
and he has given you his gun.
Trust this man, and trust his guns;
they will lift you from your dust and bring you back.
But beware of all other white men; most of all,
the dogs dressed in gray cloth and iron,
these men of God will steal your hunting grounds and kill
    your game.
When you fire your gun at them,
their fallen bodies will be like a stairway
of white rock for you to walk on.

MORTON

Bring out the barter.

> [*Two Englishmen bring out guns and kegs of powder.* ASSA-
> WAMSET *makes a lordly gesture and Indians bring out a pile
> of furs*]

ASSAWAMSET

I make you a sachem of the Narraganset.

MORTON

You are my brother.

7

ASSAWAMSET

[Lifts his hand and a young INDIAN GIRL *comes to him]*

I give you my daughter.

MORTON

You are my brother and my father.
One blood, one life.

ASSAWAMSET

No longer than our life.

The scene

In the 1630's, Merry Mount, the settlement of Thomas Morton near Wollaston, Massachusetts.

To one side, a Maypole covered with fresh birch branches and tied with ribbons of twenty different colors. In the background, a little to one side, the front of a brown seventeenth-century house with diamond windows. A small group of REVELLERS is trying on animal heads: wolves, stags, etc. In the middle ground, a fine young man with a rainbow scarf; with him, a beautiful woman in a rainbow-colored dress. They are EDWARD and EDITH, just married and chosen King and Queen of the May, for it is the First of May. A MAN comes out and sloppily attaches a flag, the Red Cross of England, above the doorway. In the foreground, two men are talking. They are THOMAS MORTON, the head of the settlement, and MR. BLACKSTONE, an Episcopal minister, just arrived from England. MORTON wears a shabby coffee-colored suit, part cloth and part deerskin. He is overweight and his manner with the minister is complacent, oily and conciliatory. MR. BLACKSTONE is dressed in a finely fitting black minister's habit. He has long set cavalier hair and talks with the crisp briskness of a high official addressing an inferior.

MR. BLACKSTONE

I don't know why I am here at Merry Mount.

These hills don't look like hills; they are too blue;
the ocean is even bluer,
there are three thousand miles of it between me and home,
between here and Oxford and my King.
I wonder why he picked me for this mission.

MORTON

We are strange co-conspirators, your Reverence.

MR. BLACKSTONE

I don't understand you, Mr. Morton.

MORTON

I mean we are in this together, your Reverence.

MR. BLACKSTONE

I suppose we'll have to work together.
I wonder why Archbishop Laud chose me.
I am a specialist in Church of England ritual.
This is my first taste of exile and authority.

MORTON

Bite on it! Our love of authority
is the only appetite that grows fiercer with age.

MR. BLACKSTONE

I'll never love this new world.
I'm used to prepared ground. Back in England,
the fields are already golden for the harvest. I was trained
to put the final polish on a parish that was already shining.

MORTON

This is the *new* England, this is God's land.
That's why it's so rough;
even the Puritans can't change that.

If you stay here in Merry Mount, and open your eyes,
    you'll love it.
Look at me, I know its animals, its birds,
and every inch and inlet of this coast,
as far south as Plymouth and as far north as Salem.

MR. BLACKSTONE

I'm not a bird watcher or an Indian, Mr. Morton.
I don't see the point of this outpost.

[*Distant gunshot*]

. . . Life hangs on a hair here.

MORTON

There's money in it. Money and renewal!
Come down to earth with us, sir! I felt as you do when I
    first came here:
no noblemen, cathedrals or plays. But you'll get used to us.
I need you officially. I want you to crown
Edward and Edith King and Queen of the May.

MR. BLACKSTONE

I have just married them, that's as far as my office goes.
I have serious work to do, Mr. Morton!

MAN WITH STAG'S HEAD

[*In a high comical voice*]

We need the priest of God to give us our true king
    and queen.

REVELLERS

Give us a king and queen.

11

MORTON

You see how much we want you.

EDWARD

Make me a king, your Holiness!

MR. BLACKSTONE

A true king rules by divine right,
he is born king, not made one by the clergy.
Thank God, we no longer live in the bad old days
of the prophet Elishah, a king-maker and a killer!

[*Wearily*]

Come, Edward, I crown you May King.
Edith, I crown you May Queen.

EDWARD

We are here.

EDITH

Life will never be as good as it is.

EDWARD

We are at Merry Mount, here in the wilderness.

EDITH

Yes, Eden gone before it began.

REVELLERS

Hurrah for King Edward and Queen Edith!
Hurrah for the King and Queen of England!

MR. BLACKSTONE

Now that the coronation is over,
I hope you will excuse me. I have reports to write for
    the Crown.

MORTON

[*Turning and catching the hand of* ASSAWAMSET'S *daughter*]

I have another marriage in mind.

MR. BLACKSTONE

Whose?

MORTON

[*Putting his arm around the girl*]

Ours.

MR. BLACKSTONE

When?

MORTON

Today, tomorrow, maybe never.

MR. BLACKSTONE

Choose never. You may want to return to England.
It's a heartache and an unkindness
to saddle these savages with our flesh and sacraments.
I must leave you. I have reports to write for the Crown.

[MR. BLACKSTONE *starts to go*]

MORTON

Why, Mr. Blackstone, you are neglecting your parish!
My children are breaking in the wilderness for you.

[*In a loud voice*]

Put on your heads, my children,
and be the animals you are.
Dance round and round the Maypole,
and show our pastor what life is made for.

[Reads in a buffoonish singsong while the REVELLERS *put on their animal heads and dance obscenely around the Maypole]*

I've whiskey and gin
to make your heads spin,
like a drumming drum
or a barrel of rum,
when the King and Queen come.
I've wolves and stags
and men in rags
to kiss the long throat
and beaver coat
of any free maid,
be she white or red,
laid in the forest, or laid in bed . . .

[A few WHITE *and* INDIAN GIRLS *dance onto the stage]*

MR. BLACKSTONE

Enough, Mr. Morton!
This sort of thing won't do!

MORTON

You're right, your Reverence! My verses grate
on the ear of a man trained on Virgil and the holy psalms.
You'll smooth them.

MR. BLACKSTONE

You misunderstand me, Mr. Morton!
I wasn't sent here by his Lordship of Canterbury
to smooth up your animated doggerel.
We can use the Indians to tame the Puritans,
but there must be some decency, some boundary
between the King's savage and his more civilized subjects.

Our bishops are busy working out a suitable formula
to express the King's wishes in this matter.
All this shaggy clowning and disorder must stop, sir,
or our royal patronage will be withdrawn.

MORTON

Right you are, your Reverence. This is easily fixed.

[*In a loud voice*]

Children, I want you to dance like ladies and gentlemen.
Dismiss your Indian companions.
Remember you represent the King on this frontier.
Dance for England.

[MORTON *sings, this time very correctly, as the* INDIAN GIRLS
steal off and the other REVELLERS *dance a stately and sedate
dance*]

*Fair and fair, and twice so fair,
as fair as any may be,
the fairest shepherd on our green,
a love for any lady.*

[EDWARD *leads the dance*]

*Fair and fair, and twice so fair,
listen to Cupid's curse:
all they who change old love for new,
pray gods they change for worse.*

[EDITH *leads the dance*]

MORTON

England's our old love, your Reverence.
We know England will always be our old love, don't we?

MR. BLACKSTONE

A very pretty dance, Mr. Morton!
It reminds me of our masques at Oxford.
I don't like your ribaldry.
You are very changeable and double-faced here.
You should follow King Charles, even his pleasures
    are gracious.

MORTON

The world is changeable. It's like a playing card:
a king in all his theatrical pomp in front—
and what's on the other side? Black and white squares.
I am talking about battalions of soldiers.
You've got to throw those dogs a little flesh
if you want them to fight the Puritans.

MR. BLACKSTONE

Dogs, a playing card and black and white squares!
What are you saying? Our kingdom is a pyramid.
Charles Stuart stands at the top. Below him,
his subjects descend uniformly and harmoniously
down to the lowest farmer. All's in grace and proportion.
If you don't understand the principles of our pyramid,
you'll only be an obstruction to us.

MORTON

Authority is growing on you.
I have been noticing a certain distaste
and disrespect in your voice, Mr. Blackstone.
You speak to me like a slave driver of Pharaoh. This
    hurts me.
I can't grow wheat on a pyramid. I am running
    a plantation.

16

. . . It's very lonely here.
The King doesn't have friends here.

MR. BLACKSTONE

Your plantation will take care of itself, when we've
finished our pyramid.

MORTON

That's your theory. I have mine for this country.
Lords and college men are needed in England. I'm
needed here.
The King needs a man with very diverse talents here
in America.
My men are green. I have to direct every step or they
would die.
My men aren't angels. I have to keep them happy!
Tell your Archbishop to send us no more idle ornaments.
I have a plantation. I have to make it pay. I have to live,
and walk on a razor's edge between the Indians
and Governor Endecott's Puritan settlement in Salem.

MR. BLACKSTONE

Our King understands your talents, Mr. Morton.
When you return to England, you will be paid.
Here we value your loyalty, but not your advice.
Soon your troubles will be over.
I have been given powers to revoke the charter for
this colony.
The King is sending the Puritans a royal governor.

MORTON

The Puritans won't like the idea of a royal governor.

17

MR. BLACKSTONE

Poor things! Our force
will fall on them like a thunderbolt!

MORTON

I'm sure it will. I suppose there will be a bishop.

MR. BLACKSTONE

Of course, there'll be a bishop.
I see what you are hinting at—
God preserve me from such a promotion!

MORTON

Oh no, you'll be useful. You have the right presence.
You will fall on the Puritans like a thunderbolt.
I have one more question: I suppose the King
will be sending an even more useful standing army over,
a regiment or two to keep the Puritans in a good humor?

MR. BLACKSTONE

That won't be necessary.
No one disputes with a king.
Of course he has regiments to spare.

MORTON

None to spare on America, I guess;
the King needs that sort of talent in England.
I hear there's been Presbyterian trouble in Scotland.

MR. BLACKSTONE

All smoke and no fire.
You know how those dissenters like to preach.

MORTON

I never knew a man so short of cash as King Charles.
The Presbyterians don't think he's earned his taxes.

MR. BLACKSTONE

That will be over in a year or two.
I doubt if anyone will care to be a Presbyterian
when we have thoroughly installed our Church.
Every creature in the land will have his place on
    our pyramid,
each will be free to obey his proper superior.
Money will pour in like water.
Then our kingdom will pay, as you say of your plantation.

MORTON

That will be the end of the world!
. . . A king, archbishops, bishops, governor generals,
governors, clerks, offices, titles and penalties . . .
the wheels won't turn. There's no money—
Or is the Lord of Hosts your servant?

MR. BLACKSTONE

You are speaking like a dissenter.

MORTON

No, you misunderstand me. I reverence your Archbishop.
God knows, I need all the authority he can give me here at
    Merry Mount.
Do you see this book? Bishop Laud sent it to me.
It's the Book of Common Prayer. It's my Bible.
Night and day, I drum it into the heads of these animals.
I mean my children. I call these people my children.
I am their father. I love this book.
I've even tried to convert the Puritans to its
    harmonious English.
That's why they hate me, that's why they manhandle me.
They've made a hog sty of my plantation.

19

MR. BLACKSTONE

The Puritans must have something else on you
besides your love of the Book of Common Prayer.

MORTON

Well, they don't care for our May Days.
Oh, I know that May Day probably needs a proper ritual.
Your prayer book will soon include that,
but there's no harm in May Day. It's traditional,
it must come down to us from the Goths.
It's one of those things that makes England England
and survives a hundred civil wars and rulers.
You can't expect my men to change all that.
I think this might be the time for you to bless us,
and marry us to the Indians. My men have been standing
on tiptoe for months, waiting for you and this day.
All they need are a few wives to keep them
        from fornication.

MR. BLACKSTONE

Your May Day and a few other things
will have to be toned down a bit.
I can see why the Puritans wished to discipline you.
You are not suggesting that they will defy the Crown.
The King is beyond their rebellions and sermons.

        [*Wiping his forehead*]

There are flies here.

MORTON

May-flies, May-flies. I am here,
the King is beyond the sea. You think
I am the only fly in the King's butter.

Well, I probably am, but these kings,
they come and go with us.
I can't keep track of them. This one
will go like the rest, but England remains.

MR. BLACKSTONE

Would our nation still be England,
if a Puritan were King?
A man like your Governor Endecott.
I am talking foolishness,
but such revolutions have happened on the Continent.
John Calvin and John Knox—those criminal John
    the Baptists—
do they think our Christian Prince is King Herod?

MORTON

Of course they think Charles is Herod,
or Nebuchadnezzar or something of the kind,
but England will survive that little fever of faith.
We'll have men singing psalms through their noses,
and marching and countermarching through the realm
    in iron.
Then their dust will blow off. We'll have another king,
new bishops, new May Days—there'll be
license for the subject and power for the statesmen.
Our supply of both is endless.

MR. BLACKSTONE

Well, I'm not losing sleep over the Puritans.
In a year or two, our new order will be the law of the land.
King and bishop, truth and power,
one seamless robe.
Do you think Governor Endecott will defy me?

MORTON

I don't know. He might give you a kick in the ribs.
I know this, though: Endecott is an Englishman,
he carried our flag, the Red Cross of England, against
 the Spaniard.
He'll never defy England. He's as loyal there as I am.

MR. BLACKSTONE

Not much to rely on, you are both double-faced,
though, of course, I know you've only been playing
with trivial things such as theft and fornication,
while Endecott is mixed up with blasphemy and treason.
I hear he was once a courtier and man of letters,
but here he is the Puritan of the Puritans.

MORTON

Yes, he's their brass bull snorting fire.
When you've been here longer, you'll learn there are
 Puritans and Puritans;
Endecott isn't like any of them. I don't understand
how he can listen by the day to his bone-headed,
turtle-brained preachers.
He never talks much. He acts,
and all he does goes against us. What soured and
 ruined him,
I guess, was the dishonesty of holding office.
No, these Puritans will never revolt from England.
That would be walking blindfold off a plank into
 the Atlantic.
They're nothing without England.

MR. BLACKSTONE

We'll grind their necks down!

22

[*A* REVELLER *comes up to* MORTON *and places a falcon on his wrist*]

That's a fine bird you have.

MORTON

I call him Hassi. Assawamset, the chief of the Narraganset,
gave him to me.

MR. BLACKSTONE

You have fearful allies, Mr. Morton.
I prefer the hawk to the savage.

MORTON

Yes, he's like a bit of England. I miss those gentlemen I
    grew up with.
They knew all about hawks. But you underestimate
    Assawamset,
he's in love with King Charles. The only
    Englishman worth
his admiration—so he thinks. King Charles ought to
    knight him
or crown him. That would be a shrewd blow against
    the Puritans.
Assawamset is a true aristocrat, much like this hawk.
They're both practiced in graceful round-about ways
    of killing.

    [*Pause*]

I was given this bird a fortnight after I landed here.
By Christmas, I had him eating out of my hand.
Gentleness and impudence, that's how I rule man or beast.

    [*A gunshot is heard off-stage*]

MR. BLACKSTONE

What's that? I don't like the sound of guns.

MORTON

One of our local Indians. They're rather a headache.
When an Indian gets something to drink,
he blasts away at anything in sight.
We have to give them liquor and guns
to get their furs.
They're sick of beads and shells.

MR. BLACKSTONE

They ought to keep their shooting out of earshot!
Why don't you set up targets for
them on some deserted beach. I don't like explosions.

MORTON

Right again, your Reverence.
I see now how much we've always needed
a Church of England man to come to Merry Mount
and teach us how to bury our garbage. Imagine thinking
of giving the Indians targets in this game-overrun country!

MR. BLACKSTONE

[*Crisply*]

Don't snap at me, Mr. Morton. My theology
teaches me to deal sensibly with what's at hand.
We know you are at hand. We can use you,
you won't regret being used by us,
so henceforth spare me your jokes,
and excuse me. I have important reports to make.

[MR. BLACKSTONE *walks stiffly into the house*]

24

MORTON

A university man. A little off the ground.
We can use him here.
He'll claw up the Puritans.

[MORTON *sits stroking his hawk. Two* PURITAN SOLDIERS *enter, a* PRIVATE *and a* SERGEANT. *They are tremendously armed: match- locks, gray uniforms, polished iron breastplates and helmets*]

Who are you standing out there,
gaping at me in iron?
You look like Spaniards.
I've put your kind to flight in the Low Countries.
You'd better move on. I'm not keeping open house.

SERGEANT

I'm not surprised you no longer know your countrymen.
We come from Governor Endecott. We're his vanguard.
Who are you, sir?

MORTON

You come from Somerset or Bristol, don't you, Sergeant?
. . . The game's not as plentiful there as here.

SERGEANT

Where I come from means nothing in the world.
What's your name?

MORTON

I am Thomas Morton, the host of Merry Mount.
I am the big sachem here. The Narraganset
have just made me a chief.

SERGEANT

We knew you were Morton. I just wanted your
own confession.

I know too why the Indians make a white man their chief.
You have been selling them guns . . .

SOLDIER

We're here to burn your settlement down.

MORTON

I admire your stubborn desperation.
Miles Standish tried to burn me out.
It won't work now. I've cleared things in England.
If you harm me, you will be punished for treason.

SERGEANT

His Excellency, John Endecott, Governor of Salem,
is on the march here. He has more soldiers than you
        can count.
You won't be able to find your settlement when he
        leaves you.

MORTON

You roar like full-grown bears now.
I remember you when you needed my help.
You whined like bears' whelps then.
I know you Puritans. Your whiskey is plunder and profit.
Your holy thirst for my mink and beaver skins is driving
        you mad.

SERGEANT

You've been giving the Indians guns for their furs.
They've been killing our women and children.

MORTON

They were probably using your own guns.
Your hands aren't clean. Don't tell me
you got the Indians' furs from them by singing psalms!

26

SERGEANT

Look at us, we are going to treat you the way Standish
treated you. He shipped you back to England like a
　　chained ape.

MORTON

You know, Sergeant, I am beginning to take to you.
You Bristol boys know how to handle the language.
Ape's a fine old English word. I've got another one
　　for Standish!
Shrimp. You think he was a giant because you never
　　saw him.
We called him Captain Shrimp. He was about four and a
　　half feet tall.
Do you know what he did? He was in the Dutch militia.
He was such a runt they made him a drummer.
When he came here, I gave him such a welcome
he wished his drum were big enough to hide under.
He wished his drum was Diogenes' tub.

SERGEANT

Who is this Diogenes?

MORTON

He was a droning, drearily dressed fellow,
like you or Standish, only he had brains and talked Greek.
Standish caught me by creeping up on me by stealth.
Eight men to one! They were so happy at bagging me,
they called me the great dragon of the Apocalypse.
They all got drunk. I was a Trojan horse to them.
Sergeant, do you know what a Trojan horse is?

SERGEANT

We go on foot here.
How should I know about fancy Spanish horses?

MORTON

Let me tell you something:
if you ever see a Trojan horse, don't give him the keys
to Boston or Salem. He'll eat your hearts out.
Do you want to know how I tripped up Standish?
While the Puritans were drinking themselves blind,
I pretended I was sick.
I didn't eat or drink a thing.
I wanted to stay awake. I was as watchful
as the geese that guarded the Roman Capitol.
You wouldn't know about those geese, Sergeant,
you're city-bred and a Puritan.
Anyway, I was watchful. In the dead of night,
I cut loose from the stupid armed tinker
they'd tied in bed with me like a bride to hold me down.
I broke through two double-locked doors.
"What shall we do? Oh, what shall we do?
He's gone, he's gone. He's gone!"
That's how they gabbled. They ran together
like rams at full butt in the dark.
Standish was so angry he broke his breastplate,
but I was out and free and in my own country.
I knew every inch of it!

SERGEANT

I've heard they caught up with you next morning
and shipped you like a chained ape to England.

MORTON

You have apes on the brain, Sergeant!
I let them capture me because
I wanted to save their poor and worthy blood.
They came at me like a flock of geese,
or horses tailed together at a fair:
I could have knocked them down like ninepins,
but I wanted to save their English blood. I had two men,
one was dead drunk, the other was a coward.
That sort of thing won't happen here now;
we have the King and Church behind us.
We have claws!

SERGEANT

We are waiting for Governor Endecott.
He is a moderate man, perhaps he'll enjoy your stories.
We don't. The Governor has more soldiers than he
    can count.
I think he'll order them to burn your settlement to
    the ground.

MORTON

Yes, I fear his patience and moderation
more than your dull ferocity.
Come to your senses, Sergeant.
We're all Englishmen. There're few enough of us in
    the world.
There's no need for us to run berserk and kill one another.

SERGEANT

What's so English about you?

29

MORTON

My flag. Do you see it flying over my door?
I hope you'll enjoy the sight and breathe the clean air here.
I'm sorry I can't invite you into my house.
If you wait here, you may get some new ideas.
You may want to count up your soldiers, and march back
  to Salem.

[MORTON *goes into house*]

SERGEANT

Morton has missed his calling. He should have been
  a preacher,
then we would have had to listen.

SOLDIER

Yes, sir, but let me warn you.
You are talking too much about the numbers of
  our soldiers.
God is a host.
If we only had eyes to see,
we would see the heavenly chariots and battalions
hovering about us. Here in America, we are in Israel,
where the breath of faith
blew down the walls of Satan.

SERGEANT

Chariots? How long do you think they'd stand up to
  our gunfire?
We've got something better than a heavenly host.
We have Endecott. He's lucky to have a man
with my war experience and black tongue
to beat some shape into you dreamers and meeting-
  house orators.

30

SOLDIER

The battlefield is only the great meeting house.
Have you noticed the Governor lately?

SERGEANT

Of course.

SOLDIER

Have you noticed how he keeps whining to himself,
and complaining about his armor?
First it's too light, then it's too heavy.
Then he keeps jumping from subject to subject.
I can't follow a man unless he stays on one subject.

SERGEANT

You should go on dreaming about the heavenly host,
and leave the Governor alone.
He'll do our thinking for us.

SOLDIER

He has been doing too much thinking.
Do you think he'll burn this settlement?

SERGEANT

No.

SOLDIER

I think the Governor is turning away from God.
No one gets killed any more.
I tell you, a man must live by faith in this colony.

SERGEANT

Don't worry about the Governor's faith.
He's a man much like me, only educated.
These things are over your head, soldier;

running a colony takes a lot of juggling.
He still keeps a loaded pistol in his right hand
and a Bible in his left. We've just killed
the chief of the Narraganset, Assawamset. What more do
     you want?

SOLDIER

Remember how the Lord turned away from Saul
for sparing the Amalekites. What are we doing here?

SERGEANT

This is a war.

> [*More shots are heard off-stage. The* REVELLERS, *terrified and
> with torn clothes, are herded in by the* PURITAN SOLDIERS. *One
> of the* SOLDIERS *is an Indian, half in war paint, half in armor.*
> GOVERNOR ENDECOTT *comes last. He is a sad, resolute man, with
> a grizzled beard that covers the upper part of his burnished
> breastplate. A* SOLDIER *follows him and carries the Red Cross
> standard of England. The* SOLDIERS *ground their matchlock
> butts on the stage and form lines*]

ENDECOTT

Men, I congratulate you:
on the march from Salem to here, you've kept step
     like Spaniards,
you've moved as fast as cavalry.
There's not much here for you,
just a mob of vicious men and women . . .
women and men dressed up as women.
Putting them down will be child's play for you,
but I want you to show that we are humble,
show that we are obedient, show that we are mighty.
We have borne the Red Cross of England to Merry Mount.

SERGEANT

[*Pointing to flag over doorway*]

Here's another flag just like it, your Excellency.

ENDECOTT

There are flags and flags.
This one at Merry Mount sags pretty badly.
It bulges in the belly.
I wish these people had a little iron in them,
then we could show how we handle our weapons.
Lead them before me.
For lack of a better,
I am the arm of God here, Sergeant.

SERGEANT

Here's a fellow gotten up as a wolf, sir.

MAN WITH WOLF'S HEAD

Spare me, your Excellency!
I put on this wolf's head to amuse my children.
I was playing the wolf in the fables.
I have never touched flesh.

ENDECOTT

This is no wolf! If he had fangs,
I'd drive a spike through his tongue and brain,
and hang him under that flag,
let his blood spill down the steps.
This fellow is an old ewe sheep pretending he's a wolf.
We'll stick him in the pillory.
He can howl and grin there till sunset.

[*A pillory is brought out. The* MAN *is put in it*]

33

SERGEANT

Here's a fellow gotten up as a stag, sir.
What shall we do with him?

MAN WITH STAG'S HEAD

Spare me, your Excellency!
I saw the white May blossoms falling,
thought they were snow, and changed to a reindeer.
I am bearing gifts to the Indians.
I am a Christmas reindeer.

ENDECOTT

Put halters on his neck and break him in like a mule.
He is used to bringing cheer,
let him drag my gun carriage.

[*Halters are put on the* STAG MAN. *He drags a cannon across the stage.* MR. PALFREY, *a young Puritan Minister, enters, brisk and out of breath. He wears a black cloak, a high-crowned hat, his shoes are bemired*]

Welcome back to us, Mr. Palfrey;
I thought you had deserted me for Governor Winthrop
    of Boston.

PALFREY

I come from burying my father-in-law, Judge Bowden.
I am here to avenge him. I bring you the prayers of the
    widow and orphans.
When I heard about your march against the Indians,
the spirit of the Lord descended on me,
my feet hardly touched the ground, my shoes had wings.
The murderers must die!

34

ENDECOTT

The Judge was a somber and noble gentleman.
He pressed the Indians more than was required, perhaps.
I never thought one could kill him.

PALFREY

Age unhinges the bravest and subtlest of minds.
Judge Bowden came to believe that he had at last broken
    the Indians.
He vainly sent his unarmed sons out to plant pumpkins.
He was sitting in the sunlight of his doorway,
with his gun cradled between his knees, and reading
from his favorite book of the Bible, the conquest
    of Canaan.
He was much troubled that the Lord would strike him
    for being
too fierce with the Indians, or too gentle.
He thought he was safe. The land was cleared
for a hundred yards before his door. No arrow could
    reach him.

ENDECOTT

He was changing to a man of peace. He was no fool, though.

PALFREY

How could he know that Morton had strengthened the
    savages with guns?
One of them fired from behind a tree, creased his skull,
and stunned him. Then the cowardly skunks rushed in,
stinking and howling. They pushed the Judge into an
    elbow chair
by a long table. They took his own sword,

and sliced him across the breast and the belly.
With each stroke, they screamed, "Judge Bowden,
    Judge Bowden,
I cross off my account!" They cut off his nose and ears,
and shoved them in his mouth. They made him chew,
then they let him fall on his sword.
His wife saw it all. The Indians were too drunk on
    Morton's rum
to find where she was hiding. The Indians have tortured
    and killed
the just man, now thousands will die for the mercy of God.
I am here to help you on this angry day.

ENDECOTT

You are late, Mr. Palfrey, I fear you are too late.
We decided in our wisdom that Assawamset,
the chief of the Narraganset, was the murderer of your
    father-in-law.
We had to name someone. We had to name the man
    we wanted.
I weep for Judge Bowden. By his death, God rest his soul,
he gave us a chance to strike terror into the hearts of
    the Indians.
Assawamset is dead. I had to have him killed.
Now no Indian will stir for twenty years.
Now our necessary massacre is over. You're not
    needed here.
We missed you on the day of deliverance in Salem.
Your thirst would have been satisfied.

PALFREY

I was burying my father-in-law and mourning for him.

ENDECOTT

No, you should have been at Salem and rejoicing.
It was a great day. Many said it was the best
they'd seen since we came to New England.
Hundreds of Indians were kneeling before us on the
    town green.
Many wished to be baptized. Most of these we spared.
Then Mr. Peters began with a brief prayer,
then Mr. Marshall prayed for a large two hours,
confessing our sins in a most tragic and prudent way,
then Mr. Arrowsmith preached for an hour,
then we sang a psalm by Mr. Wigglesworth,
then Mr. Palmer preached for an hour,
then Mr. Wilson prayed for two hours,
then we sang Mr. Wigglesworth's "Oh God, We
    Praise You."
Yes, it was a glorious day. Before it ended,
I felt I was walking in my sleep through the darkness of
    our salvation.
I was carrying too much armor. My bones were like chains.

PALFREY

I am here to raise your heart.

ENDECOTT

It needs no raising. My work is done.
You should never have abandoned Governor Winthrop.

PALFREY

Mr. Winthrop is a strict man, your Excellency,
a deliberating man, but after I'd ministered to him,
I wished to be at your side and in the line of battle.

There is no man like you. When you march,
you set the earth on fire.

ENDECOTT

I suppose I can use your angry voice,
but there'll be no fire. This is routine police work.
You need something stronger to sink your teeth into,
but I've nothing to give you.

PALFREY

You are still Endecott. You'll never shrink
into a lawyer and philosopher like Winthrop.

ENDECOTT

Oh, no, I have grown much like Governor Winthrop.
Too much administration makes a man thoughtful
        and hesitant.
After this last expedition, I felt the food inside me
was thickening to mud. I go to sleep on duty.
My armor is too heavy. My bones are burning.

PALFREY

You are a sleeping lion, sir. You must destroy
        Merry Mount.
Then you can administer in peace and be wise as Solomon.

SERGEANT

Here's a young man gotten up as a witch,
your Excellency. What shall we do with him?

MAN DRESSED AS A WITCH

    [*In an old woman's falsetto*]

I am anointed with the juice of smallage,

cinquefoil, wolf-bane, and the fat of a newborn babe.
I'm out to catch young men going to communion.

PALFREY

I know this babbler, your Excellency.
He is as blasphemous here as in Boston.
Jam a cleft stick on his tongue,
and let him gag till his tongue drops off.

ENDECOTT

Oh, angry voice! God has spoken, Sergeant.
Fasten a twig to this fellow's tongue
and let him munch till sunset.

[*A stick is put in the* YOUNG MAN's *mouth*]

SERGEANT

Here's an Indian girl, your Excellency.
We caught her dancing with the English people.
She doesn't know a word of English.

ENDECOTT

God be praised, I won't have to speak to her or hear her.
I feared she was a white woman dressed as a heathen.

PALFREY

She may know no English, but Englishmen know *her*
    well enough.
She is a whore. Heat up a poker, Sergeant,
then burn a red *A* on her red cheeks!
This isn't the court of the Archbishop
who blesses such abominations!

ENDECOTT

God has spoken again, Sergeant.

Bring out an apron with an *A* sewn on it,
and let it dangle from the girl's neck.

> [*An apron is put on the* GIRL's *neck. An arrow from off-stage
> falls at* ENDECOTT's *feet. He breaks it contemptuously, and kicks
> it away with his armored foot*]

This is like David coming out against Goliath with
    a slingshot,
only with far different results. We have collected
    their guns,
now their toy arrows pop off our steel caps and breastplates
like shuttlecocks. I feel ridiculous,
standing here enclosed in iron.

PALFREY
They may seem like toys to you, sir,
but these arrows have killed our English men and women,
they have even caught full-grown men off guard.
Look ahead of us, your Excellency, look onward.
We face three thousand miles of wilderness;
each mile is held by a savage tribe—enough solid land
to fill up the sea from here to England.
We must liberate our land from strangers,
even if each mile is a marsh of bodies.

ENDECOTT
Oh, there's little hope of that, sir.
None of these Indians will make a stand against us.
Now that their chief is gone, they hardly give us
a day of real soldiering in a year's marching.
Here, Sergeant, take four men and round up
the Indians . . . Morton's camp followers!

[*The* SOLDIERS *march off.* PALFREY *and* ENDECOTT *advance to the front of the stage. The lights begin to darken*]

I still feel I am walking in my sleep through the darkness.
If I could crawl out of my armor . . . I might be
    alive then.

PALFREY

I am a much older and weaker man than you are,
your Excellency. But nothing holds me back
when the Lord's work is waiting.
On a day like this, you mustn't crawl on your belly,
you must stand, you must stamp on this wasp's nest.
Then you can rest. Why do you water down
    my punishments?

ENDECOTT

Have you ever seen a hollow suit of armor walking, or
    trying to walk?

PALFREY

I've never seen such things, nor hope to;
only the Catholics and the heathen see visions.
Why do you wander so and avoid my questions?
You are un-Christian, sir, to soften my punishments.

ENDECOTT

Look, I am the hollowness inside my armor.

PALFREY

Please, come back to us, sir!

ENDECOTT

I have had the fevers lately,

I have been thinking too much about my dead wife.
She used to enjoy dancers like these in England.

PALFREY

God gives, and God takes.

ENDECOTT

I have read something of the sort,
but never so tersely expressed.
Come! We are old comrades. I want to speak to
    you honestly.
I have been having the fevers. In my fever,
I seem to be pacing in chains through a strange land.
I keep thinking they will rust away, or my flesh . . .

PALFREY

It's dangerous to peer into our own minds,
your Excellency. When I am bewildered,
I make my mind a blank and read the Bible.
Then the Lord fills my emptiness with wisdom.

ENDECOTT

I know, I know. I am an old admirer of your sermons.
But, you see, in my fever I kept asking myself
questions and questions, things no man in authority
has ever answered. When my wife died, I served in
    the army.
Somehow, I found I couldn't stomach killing
without an iron faith. I found that iron faith.

PALFREY

The iron of the Lord is more precious than gold.

ENDECOTT

I got little gold . . . then I came here.

Listen closely to me. I am making
a confession, and at the same time giving
you a little lesson in statecraft.
When I came here, I found my training
had only prepared me to be the colony sheriff.
My job was peacetime police work,
not the sort of thing a soldier could take much pride in.
At first, my administration was rough and quick.
I did things no Englishman would suffer,
but no more than a frontier colony demands.

PALFREY

I have honored you above all our officers and preachers.
Now you need prodding.

ENDECOTT

No, I needed thoughts, but none of you could help.
When I was working and struggling with the government
of King Charles, I found that each action
I wished to take had to be reconsidered in the light
of a report to England. Costly, influential
royal officials had to be persuaded or bribed.
All my decisions had to be such as could be described
not only in my letters but in my enemies' letters
as pleasing the King. Pleasing the King! By my soul,
I never proposed or believed in submission.
I have learned to procrastinate and wait on Providence.

PALFREY

You make problems where there are none.
Say what you believe, believe what you say.
Statecraft is quite over my head.

ENDECOTT

Yes, it's quite unlike the clean invigorating air of
     your pulpit.
I found there were ways of crying out and lifting
my armed hand, then letting it drop without bloodshed.
I found ways of letting sinners slip through my hands.
I found I had returned to my old self . ∴ .
The selves we were when my young wife and I
were at the court of the old King.
My black Puritan shadow still darkens the land.

PALFREY

Even in these last erring days, we honored you
above all others. We trusted the Lord would
     give substance
to your shadow.

ENDECOTT

No, you haven't heard. This question is insoluble.
While I was hedging and compromising,
I was in a state of chronic fever, enough
to dizzy me, not enough to keep me from marching.
I began to see that men are twisted,
that nothing is clear,
as King Charles and Archbishop Laud believe.
Look, my hand is puffed and twisted with heat . . .
Well, bearing with diseases is the body's fortune.

PALFREY

God forbid that we believe
what Archbishop Laud believes.

44

ENDECOTT

Ah, but you see, you do speak like the Archbishop:
one Church, one creed, one priesthood.
Each city is a Jerusalem:
Rome, Geneva, London, and now Boston and Salem.
I wonder what I am doing here.
Flags of a hundred colors,
they're all made of cloth.

PALFREY

There's one faith and one flag.

ENDECOTT

Listen to me. I had a dream last night.
It will interest you.
You are in it, Palfrey.
It has a pastoral simplicity:
green pastures, sheep and sky. Something a-fire.

PALFREY

This foretells the burning of Merry Mount.

ENDECOTT

No, I was sick with fever. This burning
was only in my brain, in my dream . . . I was you there,
I was preaching from your pulpit in Salem.
I was an apotheosis of you, much grander,
much more royal, more like a Jesuit general.
I was reading black sentences on the black page
of a ribboned book. I had on black horn glasses
    without lenses.
And read from a book whose print I couldn't see.
Behind me sat an old man—

I think he was Almighty God.
He looked like a dirty old Italian Pope.
A yellow slop, like corn meal, oozed from the corner of
    his mouth.
I was sorry God had fallen on bad times,
but when I read my sentence, his ringed finger
dropped trembling with approbation on my shoulder,
and I shivered with fever and rapture.

PALFREY

You were mortally sick,
but I think you were reading the words of God.

ENDECOTT

No, each time I read a sentence,
I was sentencing a man to death!
Men! I was sentencing men, not sinners!
But at first there weren't any men.
I was staring at the blank glass window of your church,
empty blue sky, empty sheep, an empty field.
Something was burning. The air was full
of black flakes, like bits of your black coat.
I saw the church crowded with our own Boston and
    Salem people:
Winthrops, Dudleys, Welds, Peterses!
I knew all the names. I could see so close, I could even see
    the insides of their houses.
I was dressed in black and white like you.
They were dressed in black and white.
I held my hands over them to bless them,
but my heart hurt inside me like the ball of the sun,
because I was sending them out to be burned.

46

PALFREY

No more, no more.

ENDECOTT

In the end, when I had cleared the church,
my own soldiers were dragging each other off.
I saw their armor melting down like lead.

PALFREY

[*Kneeling*]

Look, I am kneeling before you.
You must join me and take comfort.

ENDECOTT

In the end I was the only man in the world,
I was alone and I wasn't even myself.
I was you, or some other preacher.
I felt my heart soaking through my ribs
like the brown juice of a crushed grasshopper.

PALFREY

Join me.

ENDECOTT

I was hacking thistles
with the crude sort of sickle we make in America.
I hit so awkwardly that two
thistles grew up for each one I mutilated.
Then I was hitting men with an ax.
It was a warped American ax; it hit askew.

PALFREY

Kneel!

47

ENDECOTT

[*Still standing*]

Two sprang up for each I felled.
I couldn't kill them.
Green grass, blue sky; and in all that vacancy,
our flag, the Red Cross, was knocking and hacking in
    the wind.

PALFREY

Kneel!

ENDECOTT

[*Kneeling*]

All men will surely die, my God,
but you live forever.

[*Pause.* ENDECOTT *slowly gets to his feet*]

My mind is clear now. I don't believe in evil dreams
any more than you do, but I now understand statecraft:
a statesman can either work with merciless efficiency
and leave a desert;
or he can work in a hit-and-miss fashion,
and leave a cesspool.
Still, things aren't really bad here yet,
the King hasn't settled on his final course of action;
I can still delay, evade, pull the strings.

PALFREY

You are talking statecraft. This is over my head.

ENDECOTT

We are drawing the noose tight about our necks.

48

Still, things aren't really bad yet.
That time will come, that time will surely come—
I knew the King's mind, or rather the minds of
    his advisers—
kings can't be said to have minds.
The King will revoke our charter,
he will quarter soldiers on us,
he will impose his church system.

PALFREY

How can King Charles revoke our charter?
He signed it with his own hand.
He is evil, but how can a king break his word?

ENDECOTT

The word of a king, the word of a king!
He dare not do anything else. Listen,
if you could hear across the ocean, you would hear
the grinding of the mill. We are the grinding.

PALFREY

Oh, God, have mercy on us!
All our labors here will perish.
What will we do? What will we do?

ENDECOTT

You will do nothing. You will cave in.
You will give in to King Charles, even if he asks for
    your lives.
Do you think that I, too, will do nothing?
I have little faith. The faith of the armies.
I am only alive when I am fighting for my life.
I detest this, but it is so.

49

My ax can never be taken from me.
My hand, my bare hand, is an ax.
I will speak.

PALFREY

You will speak?

ENDECOTT

[*Thinking to himself*]

It will be a hollow, dishonest harangue,
half truth, half bombast.
But let's hope every word will be practical.
It must stir soldier and preacher to fury.
Then—no toleration, no quarter!
Everything here in America will be Bible, blood and iron.
England will no longer exist.

PALFREY

I don't understand what you mean by "England will no
longer exist."
Will our new commonwealth still exist without England?

ENDECOTT

For us, there will be only a
brief moment when our commonwealth will say,
"I am," then shut her eyes to the world.
Sooner or later, we will go. Perhaps it will be soon,
perhaps the King will send over an army,
or the French will move down from the north,
or the Dutch will move in from the south.
Sooner or later, today, tomorrow or the day after,
we will be gone. I will rejoice then,

50

if I can say I've had my black second
of anguish and exultation.

[*The stage lightens. Sounds of returning soldiers*]

PALFREY

Our soldiers are coming back.
You are tired, your Excellency.
Shall I speak for you and judge the prisoners?

ENDECOTT

You can announce any judgments you like.
I will stand behind you
and qualify them.

[*The* SERGEANT *and* SOLDIERS *march back on stage, dragging
three hysterical and drunken* INDIANS. *A* SOLDIER *holds three
broken bows.* PALFREY *and* ENDECOTT *walk back and look at
the prisoners*]

SERGEANT

I threw two men out in front to make a noisy show,
then marched my two others around the Indians' flank.
Maurice of Nassau's trick. I caught the Indians in a vise.
What shall we do with them, your Excellency?

ENDECOTT

Take over, Preacher Palfrey. We will have a practical
exhibition of theocracy in action.

PALFREY

Take the Indians out of sight
and shoot them. This plague must be smothered
if we want our children to live in freedom.

ENDECOTT

The man of God has spoken:
Take the Indians out of sight!
There's an icehouse in this settlement, isn't there?
Throw the Indians into the icehouse,
and let them sober up on sawdust.

[*A* BEAR *in pink stockings comes out. He dances and paws the air absurdly in front of* ENDECOTT *and* PALFREY]

SERGEANT

What shall we do with this beast, sir?
Shall we strap him to a post and whip him?

PALFREY

A dancing bear! He is against nature!
He must be a witch. Shoot him in the head!

ENDECOTT

Shoot the damned bear in the head, Sergeant!

[*The* SERGEANT *shoots the* BEAR. *It dies with antic gestures. The* SERGEANT *then leads out* EDITH *and* EDWARD *in their rainbow costumes*]

SERGEANT

Here's the King of the May and his wife.
They are young and shining. What shall we do with them?

PALFREY

Strap the King to a whipping post,
and give him twice as many lashes as the others.
His high station should set an example.

EDWARD

Speak like an Englishman, sir.

If my hands were free, I'd fight you off till you killed me;
I don't ask mercy for myself,
but pray you not to touch my bride.
We were just married.

PALFREY

We'll give her something to remember her wedding
     day by!
We are not in the habit of wasting idle courtesies
     on women.
We're twice as strict with women.
Sergeant, tie the King and Queen to a whipping post.

ENDECOTT

Slowly, Mr. Palfrey, slowly.
Weddings and birth . . .

     [*Dreamily putting a hand on* EDITH's *shoulder*]

You are too young, but that's no disadvantage in a wife.

EDITH

Is your own wife in Salem, Governor Endecott?
She should come here and soften your judgment.

ENDECOTT

What would my wife be doing in Salem?
She was a lovely and intelligent lady
who died twenty-five years ago.
Our child died with her.

EDITH

So you became a great Puritan.

ENDECOTT

     [*Puts his hand on* EDITH *again*]

You are almost as beautiful . . .
Misfortune has fallen too early on you and your husband.
You will have time to mend. Your husband looks
as if he could handle a matchlock in our militia.
You will come to Salem. You will probably bear children.
I hope they will live.

> [ENDECOTT *walks slowly away, as if dreaming, then turns, picks
> up a large rose garland, and lays it over the heads of* EDITH *and*
> EDWARD. *He pauses, then in a loud voice*]

Sergeant, march the King and Queen off,
then disrobe them and give them something practical
    to wear.

PALFREY

Shouldn't the King's curled hair be cropped?

ENDECOTT

The voice of divine inspiration has spoken.
Sergeant, cut the King's hair off
in our attractive pumpkin-shell style!

> [EDITH *and* EDWARD *are led off*]

PALFREY

> [*Angrily*]

Your Excellency!

ENDECOTT

What was I to do, friend?
They are children.

PALFREY

Cleopatra and the Pope were children once.

54

I know all I want to about such children.
Remember Michael Wigglesworth's lines on
  unbaptized children.
These are worse than unbaptized.

  [*Sings in a nasal voice*]

  Then to the bar they all drew near
  who'd died in infancy;
  they never had or good or bad
  effected pers'nally,
  but from the womb into the tomb
  had dropped like rotten seed.
  No child had sinned, each child was damned;
  they thus began to plead:

  "If for our own transgression
  and disobedience,
  we here must stand on your left hand,
  just were the recompense;
  but Adam's guilt our souls has split,
  his fault is charged upon us,
  and that alone has overthrown
  our spirit and undone us."

  Then God replied, "You sinners are,
  and sinners shall expect
  such as they'll get, for I do save
  none by my own elect."

  [MORTON, *partly drunk, but more in a state of despairing reck-*
  lessness, reels onto the stage with his arm around the INDIAN
  GIRL. *He stands defiantly staring at the Puritans*]

MORTON

Very edifying verses, Minister. I don't know
which to admire more, your art or your morality.
Look, I'm a poet too.

[*Squeezes the* INDIAN GIRL]

This is my poetry. We are your elect.
The lamb will lie down with the lion.

PALFREY

I know your poetry. The murder of my father-in-law
was another of your compositions. You'll wish you'd stuck
    to words
and filthy songs, when we crop your ears,
and bore your nose, and burn your house.

SOLDIER

We found Morton behind a tree;
he had a gun slanting on his knees.
He was afraid to use it.

MORTON

Everyone in this colony knows, your Excellency,
I can hit a turkey's head off at fifty yards.
I could have shot you down any time in the last half hour.
While you were posturing back and forth and talking to
    your preacher,
I was sitting in the dark of my house,
and my gun was pointing at you.
Then this Indian lady came along and gave me
something stronger to think on than killing.

PALFREY

Hand Morton over to me. I'm trained for this.

I'll offer the criminal to the mercies of God.
You will hear no more of him.

MORTON

You ought to be in your own pillory of a strait jacket,
you homicidal Bible-mangling donkey.
I stand here to address his Excellency,
John Endecott of Salem.

ENDECOTT

Morton, you are a foolish and swollen man
with little future, and in that little, little to be envied;
but it seems I owe my life to your debaucheries.
Do you know that I am going to suppress your settlement?
Think quickly. Your plantation is still standing.

MORTON

Governor Endecott,
we are both Englishmen. We were both gentlemen once.
We have both carried the flag of England against
        the Catholics.
I call on you to treat your brothers in arms with honor,
and allow us our legal rights.

ENDECOTT

This is the first time I've heard of your campaigning,
        Mr. Morton.
I am destroying you for selling whiskey and firearms to
        the Indians.
Your Indians imperil my colony.

MORTON

This is a legal and civil question, Mr. Endecott.
Our courts in England will settle it.

57

I am a lawyer myself. I have other good lawyers in my pay.
You'll make little headway in England.
It'll be my word against your word, witness
    against witness.
Of course, I know why you hate me. You hate me
for belonging to our apostolic Church of England,
for my devotion to our Book of Common Prayer.
I love that book.

ENDECOTT

Mr. Morton,
your church and reading habits are neither here nor there.
I am here to enforce moral decorum.
Your May Days, they seem to come up once a month, are
    a horror.
Your diseased men drink themselves insensible,
and live with Indian women. Look,
your mixed creatures, half white, half red,
like our flag, are spreading through our colony.
We cannot last.

MORTON

Our May Days are lovely and human,
they are a beautiful old English custom
practiced by your ancestors and mine, Mr. Endecott.
You Puritans walk in blinders.
You look neither to the left nor to the right.
You are only interested in trade.
You beat up my Indians because
they sell me the furs they refuse to sell you . . .

ENDECOTT

This is getting nowhere.

You are repeating yourself.
You are losing your sense of sequence and logic.
For your own health I will have to have you gagged.

MORTON

You know, I don't think you will have me tied or gagged.
Do you know who this lady is?
She is the daughter of Assawamset, the great chief of
    the Narraganset,
my blood brother. Perhaps, I'll marry her. You can't
    stop me!

[MORTON *draws the girl to him, hugging her defiantly*]
[ENDECOTT *stares at* MORTON, *stunned and confused, pauses, as
if trying to hold down a burst of hysterical fury*]

ENDECOTT

No, let her rest here for the moment.

MORTON

I know what you want, but doubt if you do.
You think you are the arm of God here,
and wish you could fold that arm around this woman.
You have a beautiful faith, one that leaves you free
to kill the Indians and steal their lands and furs,
but not free to sleep with their women.

ENDECOTT

God knows what we want or will have here.
Many things, many things . . .
Faith might have kept us clean and free—
yes, we thought that was possible for us once.
Each day drags the day before it on stage,

all its contrived and worried plot.
No one is too clean or free.

MORTON

I am myself and nothing else, when I look on this
      red woman,
but you'll never be free to trust your eye.
Poor Endecott, you are far from home,
an ocean and fifty years away.
Remember old
Charles V. Charles got his fill
of running the Holy Roman Empire and retired to
      a monastery.
I guess he didn't do much praying there,
because people found him staring at three
      unassembled clocks.
Each clock had the same vital part missing,
say the pendulum and main spring.
The Emperor kept staring at the clocks
and trying to fit them together into one perfect clock.
Of course, he couldn't, he didn't have the parts.
That taught him a lot about ruling.
I am a man of peace. My Indian allies are men of peace.
I sell them guns to keep them from starving.
I know your line. You want the Indian land.
These are innocent of blood, but you'd rather shoot them
than breed with them. You can easily shoot them all.
Then saint will live with saint. Then this continent
will be a sea of sharks.

PALFREY

Do you know how many Englishmen,

saints as you call them, we have here?

MORTON

Two or three thousand.

PALFREY

Do you know how many Indians occupy this land?

MORTON

Two or three million.

PALFREY

Do you want our stock to run out like a trickle
into the Atlantic?

ENDECOTT

We are few here, we are no thicker than a hair.

MORTON

Have no fear of their numbers. God is with you.
You can shoot them all, unless someone gives them guns.
Then God may think twice before taking sides.

ENDECOTT

Yes, I could shoot and shoot and shoot,
but I have wished to be merciful.
It's true we want the Indian lands,
but they have not been innocent.
Each time we have tried to hold back,
some new act of savage violence has forced us forward.
This new world, this world, I fear
it will be washed in blood before we can live here together.
Perhaps, when we are all dead, there'll be
a government, a just and kind government at last.

MORTON

And for the present, you are content to attack me.
Hold off. If you touch me, you'll face
the guns and knives of my blood brother, Assawamset.

ENDECOTT

Morton's guns and knives. No, I don't think so.
Assawamset is dead. I had to have him killed.

MORTON

You are lying. He was the king of the forest.
No Puritan could get to him.

ENDECOTT

After Judge Bowden's murder,
I was weary and worn and had no heart for marching,
but there was no one else to settle with Assawamset.
Then by a miracle, a day's march out of Salem,
we came on this Indian. I call him the executioner.

[*Points to the* INDIAN SOLDIER]

His brother was knifed in the back by Assawamset.
He gladly showed us where his old tribe
was encamped on an island in the swamp by Great Hope
    Neck.
I stationed my men in a circle. There was no cover;
it was scarcely possible for an Indian to escape.
Then, led by Providence,
Assawamset came out to ease himself,
naked except for his small breeches and stockings.
We fired at him, putting one bullet into his heart,
and another two inches higher.

When we fished him out of the swamp
he was a doleful, great, naked, dirty, dead beast.

MORTON

You swear he is dead. I say he is still alive.

ENDECOTT

You'll recognize his hand, I think.
It is a remarkable hand, not just for its great size,
but from being scarred all over from one
of your cheap pistols exploding in his fist.

[*Pause.* ENDECOTT *turns to the* INDIAN SOLDIER]

ENDECOTT

Executioner!

[*The* INDIAN *steps forward and throws the hand at* MORTON's *feet. The* INDIAN GIRL *gives a muffled cry, but nobody pays attention*]

That business is over.

EXECUTIONER

When I came on his body, I said,
"Assawamset, you've been a very big man,
you've made many men afraid of you.
Now big as you are, I will chop you in pieces."
I chopped him into a hundred chunks.
I got a penny for each chunk. That's all the reward I had;
except for the glory of killing our chief.

MORTON

I congratulate you, Mr. Endecott, on your proof
    of conquest.
I admire how graciously you transmute

disloyal savages into servile dissenters.
You know, I have been calling you Governor for courtesy,
but you really are no longer a governor.
That title is now as empty and hollow as your heart.
I have the king of trumps up my sleeve here,
if his Reverence will excuse me.
This is Mr. Blackstone of the Church of England.
He has a message for you from King Charles.
Speak, Mr. Blackstone, for our Church and our King!

MR. BLACKSTONE

Are you Mr. Endecott?

ENDECOTT

I am Endecott.

MR. BLACKSTONE

Mr. Endecott, I am a personal friend of Archbishop Laud.
I have had audiences with King Charles.
I am their emissary.
I hope you will realize that you are no longer talking to
    Mr. Morton.
In England, we have a systematic and dignified way
of dealing with you Puritan squires.

PALFREY

He is a man who cannot bear even the corrupt rule
of his own corrupt church!
He has come to preach evil in the wilderness,
he crowned the May King and Queen!

ENDECOTT

Let his Reverence talk, Mr. Palfrey,
he told us he was a systematic and dignified man.

64

MR. BLACKSTONE

Please attend me, Mr. Endecott.
Do you recognize that flag above our doorway?

ENDECOTT

I see the flag.

MR. BLACKSTONE

I asked you if you recognized the flag of England!

ENDECOTT

I recognize the flag of England.

MR. BLACKSTONE

I represent the flag of England in America.
In the King's name, I tell you that the King
has appointed him a tribunal for New England.
The head of the tribunal is Archbishop Laud.
Do you know Archbishop Laud, Mr. Endecott?

PALFREY

Laud is a priest of Baal!

ENDECOTT

You must excuse the Elder, Mr. Blackstone,
he is religious.
I know Archbishop Laud,
though I'm afraid I haven't the advantage of his
        personal friendship.

MR. BLACKSTONE

The tribunal for New England
has appointed a Royal Governor:
the Royal Governor will be Sir Ferdinando Gorges.
Do you know Sir Ferdinando Gorges, Mr. Endecott?

Sir Ferdinando Gorges is our arch-oppressor.
He tried to destroy our colony before we existed!

ENDECOTT
I know Sir Ferdinando, Mr. Blackstone.
We were young men at the court of King James together.
We have had legal disputes for twenty years. I think.

MORTON
I imagine you know then, Endecott,
that Sir Ferdinando and I are table companions.
We are like brothers. When he comes here as a
    Royal Governor,
I shall be at his right hand.
You had better win me over, Endecott;
my policy is to live and let live.
I am slow to anger.
You still have time.

MR. BLACKSTONE
Mr. Endecott, do you realize
that your authority and that
of Governor Winthrop of Boston and Governor Bradford
    of Plymouth
will end when Royal Governor Gorges arrives?

PALFREY
Ask to see this order in writing, your Excellency!
Tell him we will appeal to the courts in England.

ENDECOTT
You are learning statecraft, Palfrey.
I am afraid this order will be very clear.

66

And the courts of England! England has shelved
    in on us.
There is no England!

MR. BLACKSTONE

You see how easily I manage them, Morton?
I speak a few authoritative and logical words,
and they collapse. I am glad I have made myself clear
    to you,
Mr. Endecott. Our new methods have worked wonders
    in England.

ENDECOTT

Will the royal bureaucracy be imposed on New England?

MR. BLACKSTONE

You will have an orderly and systematic government,
    Mr. Endecott.

ENDECOTT

Will the discipline and ceremonial
of the Church of England be imposed on New England?

MR. BLACKSTONE

You will be given an aesthetic, rational
and systematic religion, Mr. Endecott.

ENDECOTT

You see, this is the time I told you of, Mr. Palfrey.
We have little to choose between the corruption
    of Morton
And the ruthless systematizing of Archbishop Laud.
They will give us no quarter. This is the day of terror!

PALFREY

God have mercy on us!

ENDECOTT

I will have to speak to my soldiers.

MORTON

[*Sings, like a Handel oratorio*]

Jupiter thunders,
and the Separatists burst asunder!

MAN DRESSED AS A WITCH

[*Spitting out his cleft stick*]

Quack, quack! The Governor has stolen my broomstick!
He is riding to the devil,
he thought he was riding to heaven!

MR. BLACKSTONE

You see how our new method works!

MAN WITH WOLF'S HEAD

[*From pillory*]

Let the wolves howl!

[ENDECOTT *walks slowly over to the house, climbs the steps,
then straightens and turns to the* SOLDIERS]

ENDECOTT

Sergeant, have my men form three sides of a hollow square.

SERGEANT

Form three sides of a hollow square, soldiers.

68

ENDECOTT

Have my men ground arms and stand at attention!

SERGEANT

Ground arms! Attention!

ENDECOTT

Sergeant, order the drummer to beat his drum!

SERGEANT

Drummer, beat your drum!

ENDECOTT

[*To* PALFREY]

This is a calamitous moment for us.
Give us a brief prayer.

PALFREY

May God guard and guide our Governor
in all his actions!

ENDECOTT

Soldiers—or must we be called exiles,
now that England has sunk below the horizon . . .
Look out to ocean, you will not see it;
it is invisible to us. All this long and injured day,
we have worked without words, in darkness;
and the enemy's swords and bullets have melted before us;
they are gone like ice in the breath of summer.
All this was for nothing. We, who came up from nowhere,
are sentenced to return to nowhere.
I want you to remember the country we sailed from.

69

England! England!

England, it is an excellent country,
if this can be said of a kingdom.
The Germans gave us gravity and a heart for beer;
the Normans, cruelty and reason.
In a hundred fair battles, we have stopped
the galloping French and headlong Scot.
We cracked them, then charged them to panic
        and perdition.
We have pacified their kingdoms,
and held them like slaves under our iron prong.
We have lived through civil wars,
they were prettily called the Wars of the Roses,
they were without intention or beauty;
the opposing captains were indistinguishable,
a malevolence, pressed into power by an
        unintelligible cause.
The defeated soldiers were murdered in the field,
often by their own kinsmen. That's done for.
We have closed the blood paths of the great Lords.
We have shaken off the greedy, meddling Latin Pope.
We have robbed the Spanish fleets; their hulks
        and chivalry
rot on the ocean's bottom from Cadiz to the Isthmus.
Europe sleeps in the shadow of our fear,
and England is at peace.

Perhaps your illiterate, Bible-drumming soldiers

70

need this history lesson; Mr. Blackstone and I don't.

ENDECOTT

You see our flag, the Red Cross; it still flies high;
my arms are nailed to this cross,
fighting under it for three kings and thirty years.
England still lies behind us;
it is crowded and complicated,
everything time and tradition could give a country
    is there.
I learned its customs once so that I might live.
My wife and child lie buried there.

SOLDIERS

England! England!

MORTON

This is well spoken, Mr. Endecott.

ENDECOTT

I imagine that my love and service for England
can withstand even your admiration, Mr. Morton . . .
Soldiers, I ask you why did I leave England?
Surely, it wasn't disappointment:
I was well spoken of, sought after,
and incessantly burdened with commissions in court
    and field.
You, too, according to your talent and condition,
were men of some standing in your counties;
you had cottages and fields.
I had an old stone house with servants.
Why did I come to this waste of animals, Indians, and the
    nine-month winter?

To this place that has the wildness of the whole world
        in it—
God's work, God's work, if any care, before he thought
        of life.
Boulders and tree roots have broken our plowshares,
our children have cried for bread,
we have torn mussels from the rocks to feed them.
Why did we come here?

MORTON

My children have richer food
than tree roots and mussels.

ENDECOTT

If you interrupt me again, Mr. Morton,
I'll hang you by your heels to your Maypole,
or perhaps your neck! Soldiers,
I was telling how we gave up everything.
We came here, and dared renew the world;
look about you, you will see we have painfully cleared
the true path, our rough paths to the land of promise.
Will Charles Stuart stop us? That savage,
that Scotchman, that peacock who spends more money
on clothes than any woman in the Kingdom?
Yet Charles had excellent forebears:
King James, who slobbered, his life the life of a bitch,
one uninterrupted heat for the glittering boys?
Or Queen Mary? She did what James dreamed of,
a world whore, a French agent, a common murderess,
who blew her husband up with powder.
Her death at the block shows us perhaps
        how treacherously

the Divine Will overshadows her grandson's crown.

MR. BLACKSTONE

This is treason, Mr. Endecott!
You will be sent to the Tower. You will be beheaded.

ENDECOTT

I am coming to your future, Mr. Blackstone.
Soldiers, King Charles is going to hand us over to
    Bishop Laud,
Old Thorough, our most logical persecutor.
The King and his bishops are taking counsel together.
They have appointed a Governor General.
The Governor General is going to establish
the corrupt Church of England here.
There will be a Roman bishop in every county,
a priest in every parish.

SOLDIERS

God save us from King Charles!

ENDECOTT

If the King and Bishop have their way,
there will be a cross and high altar in every
    meeting house,
a titled clerk in every office;
you will serve under good-for-nothing
    gentlemen lieutenants.
Candles will burn at noonday even on the steps to
    the pulpit.
Will you wait for this without drawing a sword?
Without firing a gun, without killing?

SOLDIERS

God save us!

ENDECOTT

No! We shall make a stand in this land,
we shall stand on this land
that we have brought our possessions to,
that we have cleared with our axes,
that we have broken with our plows,
that we have pacified with our guns,
that we have sanctified with our prayers.
God has brought us here, our manhood saves us.
What have we to do with mitred bishops?
What have we to do with anointed kings?
What have we to do with England?

SOLDIERS

What have we to do with England?

ENDECOTT

Bring me our standard,
the Red Cross of England!

SERGEANT

Yes, sir.

ENDECOTT

Sergeant, tear the Red Cross from its staff!

SERGEANT

I am afraid to. I am a soldier!
I served against Spain under this flag.

ENDECOTT

It's nothing.

74

[*Draws his sword and cuts the Red Cross from its staff. It falls to the ground at his feet*]

Before God and man, I stand by my act!
We shall have no pope or tyrant or mother country in New England!
No flag shall stand between us and our God!

SOLDIERS

No flag shall stand between us and our God!

[*They cheer* ENDECOTT. *Drums are beaten*]

MR. BLACKSTONE

This is treason and blasphemy!

ENDECOTT

Sergeant, tie up Mr. Blackstone.
Morton is quiet at last, but you'd better tie him up, too.

SERGEANT

Yes, sir.

ENDECOTT

Sergeant, take these people of Merry Mount away.

[*Pauses*]

Wait a minute. Let those people go out in their own way.
They can do their foolish May Day dance, if they must.

[*The* REVELLERS *dance the stately dance they danced previously. Their manner is quite changed, they perform pathetically and wiltingly*]

REVELLERS

Fair and fair, and twice so fair,

75

as fair as any may be,
the fairest shepherd on our green,
and love for any lady.

[EDWARD *and* EDITH *lead the dance. He is now in gray clothes and has cropped hair.* EDITH *is also dressed in gray*]

Fair and fair, and twice so fair,
listen to Cupid's curse:
all they who change old love for new,
pray God they change for worse.

ENDECOTT

This is the last masque that will be heard in New England.
Sergeant, take these people away!

SERGEANT

Yes, sir.

ENDECOTT

Then go to the icehouse and release the Indians.
Take them out in a field and shoot them!

SERGEANT

Yes, sir.

[*A* SOLDIER *takes* INDIAN GIRL *off stage*]

ENDECOTT

Sergeant, when our men are finished with the Indians,
they can start burning down the houses of Merry Mount.

SERGEANT

Yes, sir.

76

ENDECOTT

Tomorrow, we will burn the Indian village.

SERGEANT

Yes, sir.

[*The* SOLDIERS, *with the* REVELLERS, *leave.* ENDECOTT *stands alone, brooding.* PALFREY *comes up to him*]

ENDECOTT

I've made my speech and performed my act.
The earth hasn't swallowed us.

PALFREY

The earth has swallowed *them*.
What are you going to do?

ENDECOTT

I should ask for a day of mourning in the colony,
or better my own day of mourning,
for the people we have sent into misery, desperation—
that I have sent out of life:
my own soldiers, the turncoat Indians who served
        our turn,
and for the other Indians, all those who are fighting
with unequalled ferocity, and probably
        hopeless courage,
because they prefer annihilation to the despair of
        our conquest.

PALFREY

Don't look backward. Remember how Lot's wife

was turned into a pillar of salt for looking backward.

ENDECOTT

Oh, stop it, Palfrey!
You need a rest.
Go out and watch the Indians die:
they deserve the blessing of your presence.

PALFREY

Yes, your Excellency.

[As PALFREY *leaves, the* SERGEANT *comes running on*]

SERGEANT

You have given no orders for our treatment of the Merry
    Mount people.
Shall I double their punishments?

ENDECOTT

No, I don't think so.
We are burning down their houses.
I'll do something tomorrow.
Or the next day.
I will delay and wait on Providence.

SERGEANT

Yes, sir.

[He leaves the stage]

[ENDECOTT *remains alone for a few moments, head down and
brooding. He lifts the fallen Red Cross of England with his
foot. The glow of Merry Mount burns at the back of the stage.
Screams, etc.*]

ENDECOTT

I've probably already done too much . . .

[*Pause, scream*]

It's strange I was in such an unmanly terror about a flag.

[*Kicks the flag off the steps*]

It's a childish thing.

CURTAIN

MY KINSMAN,
MAJOR MOLINEUX

ORIGINAL CAST FOR

My Kinsman, Major Molineux

Premiere November 1, 1964, American Place Theatre

Robin: THOMAS J. STUBBLEFIELD

Boy (his brother): BLAISE MORTON

Ferryman: CLAYTON CORBIN

1st Redcoat: WILLIAM JACOBSON

2nd Redcoat: ROBERT TINSLEY

First Barber: JAY DOYLE

Tavern Keeper: LOGAN RAMSEY

Man with Pewter Mug: JAMES ZAFERES

Clergyman: THOMAS BARBOUR

Prostitute: SCOTTIE MACGREGOR

Colonel Greenough: TOM MCDERMOTT

Man in Periwig: HEYWOOD HALE BROUN

Watchman: JACK RYLAND

Major Molineux: GAYLORD C. MASON

Citizens of Boston: HOWARD MARTIN, LUKE ANDREAS,
    CONWAY W. YOUNG, RICHARD KJELLAND,
    SIGRUNN WAAGE, ANTONIE BECKER,
    E. EMMET WALSCH, MARTHA NEAG,
    JAMES ZAFERES, JILL MALIN, PAUL PLUMMER

The scene

Boston, just before the American Revolution.

To the left of the stage, ROBIN, a young man barely eighteen, in a coarse grey coat, well-worn but carefully repaired, leather breeches, blue yarn stockings, and a worn three-cornered hat. He carries a heavy oak-sapling cudgel and has a wallet slung over his shoulder. Beside him, his brother, a BOY of ten or twelve, dressed in the same respectable but somewhat rustic manner. On the far left of the stage, the triangular prow of a dory; beside it, a huge FERRY-MAN holding an upright oar. He has a white curling beard. His dress, although eighteenth century, half suggests that he is Charon. Lined across the stage and in the style of a primitive New England sampler, are dimly seen five miniature houses: a barber shop, a tavern, a white church, a shabby brick house with a glass bay window, and a pillared mansion, an official's house, on its cornice the golden lion and unicorn of England. The houses are miniature, but their doors are man-size. Only ROBIN, his BROTHER, and the FERRYMAN are lit up.

ROBIN

Here's my last crown, your double price
for ferrying us across the marsh
at this ungodly hour.

FERRYMAN

A crown!

Do you want me to lose my soul?
Do you see King George's face?
judging us on this silver coin?
I have no price.

ROBIN

      You asked for double.

FERRYMAN

I'll take the crown for your return trip.

    [*Takes the coin*]

No one returns.

ROBIN

      No one?

FERRYMAN

      No one.
Legs go round in circles here.
This is the city of the dead.

ROBIN

What's that?

FERRYMAN

      I said this city's Boston,
No one begs here. Are you deaf?

    [*The little houses on stage light up, then dim out*]

ROBIN

    [*To the* FERRYMAN]

Show me my kinsman's mansion. You

must know him—Major Molineux,
the most important man in town.

FERRYMAN

The name's familiar . . . Molineux . . .
Wasn't he mixed up with the French?
He's never at home now. If you'll wait
here, you'll meet him on his rounds.
All our important people drift
sooner or later to my ferry landing,
and stand here begging for the moon.
You'll see your cousin. You're well-placed.

ROBIN

I know it. My kinsman's a big man here.
He told me he would make my fortune;
I'll be a partner in his firm,
either here or in London.

FERRYMAN

       Settle
for London, that's your city, Boy.
Majors are still sterling silver across
the waters. All the English-born
suddenly seem in love with London.
Your cousin's house here is up for sale.

ROBIN

He cares for England. *Rule Britannia,*
that's the tune he taught me. I'm
surprised he's leaving.

FERRYMAN

He's surprised!
He seemed to belong here once. He wished
to teach us *Rule Britannia,* but
we couldn't get it through our heads.
He gave us this to keep us singing.

[*The* FERRYMAN *holds up a boiled lobster*]

ROBIN

You're joking, it's a lobster.

FERRYMAN

No.
Look, it's horny, boiled and red,
It is the Major's spitting image.

[*On the other side of the stage,* TWO BRITISH REDCOATS *are seen marching slowly in step with shouldered muskets.* Rule Britannia *played faintly*]

FERRYMAN

[*Pointing to* SOLDIERS]

Here are the Major's chicken lobsters.

ROBIN

Our soldiers!

FERRYMAN

We call them lobsterbacks.
They are the Major's privates. Wherever
they are gathered together, he is present.
You'll feel his grip behind their claws.

88

What are you going to do now:
run home to Deerfield, take a ship
for England, Boy, or chase the soldiers?

ROBIN

Why, I'm staying here. I like
soldiers. They make me feel at home.
They kept the Frenchmen out of Deerfield.
They'll tell me where my kinsman lives.

FERRYMAN

The French are finished. The British
are the only Frenchmen left.
Didn't you say your cousin's name
was Molineux?

ROBIN

He's Norman Irish.
Why are you leaving?

FERRYMAN

Money. The soldiers
make me pay them for the pleasure
of shuttling them across the marsh.
Run, Boy, and catch those soldiers' scarlet
coat-tails, while they're still around.

[*The* FERRYMAN *goes off pushing his boat*]
[ROBIN *and the* BOY *advance towards the* SOLDIERS]

ROBIN

I need your help, Sirs.

FIRST SOLDIER
  [*Smiling*]

    We are here
for service, that's our unpleasant duty.

  ROBIN

    I liked the way
the soldiers smiled. I wonder how
anyone could distrust a soldier.

  BOY
We've lost our guide.

  ROBIN

    We'll find another.

  BOY
Why did that boatman gnash his teeth
at Cousin Major?

  ROBIN

    He was cold.
That's how big city people talk.
Let's walk. We're here to see the city.

  [*As* ROBIN *and the* BOY *start moving, the miniature houses light up one by one and then go dark. A* BARBER *comes out of the barber shop; he holds a razor, and a bowl of suds. A* TAVERN KEEPER *enters holding a newspaper*]

BARBER

    [*Cutting away the suds with his razor*]

That's how we shave a wig.

TAVERN KEEPER
> You mean

a Tory.

BARBER
> Shave them to the bone!

TAVERN KEEPER

> [*Pointing to newspaper*]

Here's the last picture of King George;
He's passed another tax on tea.

BARBER

Health to the King, health to the King!
Here's rum to drown him in the tea!

> [*Drenches the newspaper with his mug*]
> [A CLERGYMAN, *white-wigged, all in black, comes out of the church*]

CLERGYMAN

What an ungodly hour! The city's
boiling. All's rum and revolution.
We have an everlasting city,
but here in this unsteady brightness,
nothing's clear, unless the Lord
enlighten us and show the winner!

> [*A* PROSTITUTE *comes out of the bay-window house. She wears a red skirt and a low, full-bosomed white blouse*]

PROSTITUTE

Here in the shadow of the church,

I save whatever God despises—
Whig or Tory, saint or sinner,
I'm their refuge from the church.

> [*The pillared mansion lights up. A* MAN *comes out in a blue
> coat and white trousers like General Washington's. He wears
> a grayish mask covered with pocks. His forehead juts out and
> divides in a double bulge. His nose is a yellow eagle's beak.
> His eyes flash like fire in a cave. He looks at himself in a
> mirror*]

MAN WITH MASK

My mind's on fire. This fire will burn
the pocks and paleness from my face.
Freedom has given me this palace.
I'll go and mingle with the mob.

> [*Now the houses are dark.* ROBIN *rubs his eyes in a daze, stares
> into the darkness, then turns to his brother*]

BOY

Who are these people, Brother Robin?
We're in the dark and far from Deerfield.

ROBIN

We're in the city, little brother.
Things will go smoother when we find
our kinsman, Major Molineux.

BOY

Our kinsman isn't like these people.
He is a loyal gentleman.

My Kinsman, Major Molineux

ROBIN

We'll see. He swore he'd make my fortune,
and teach you Latin.

BOY

I want something.

ROBIN

Let's see the city.

BOY

I want a flintlock.

[*A* MAN *enters from the right. He wears a full gray periwig, a
wide-shirted coat of dark cloth and silk stocking rolled up
above the knees. He carries a polished cane which he digs
angrily into the ground at every step. "Hem, hem," he says in
a sepulchral voice as he walks over to the barber shop. The
TWO BARBERS appear, ONE *with a razor, the* OTHER *with a bowl
of suds*]

MAN IN PERIWIG

Hem! Hem!

ROBIN

Good evening, honored sir.
Help us. We come from out of town.

MAN IN PERIWIG

A good face and a better shoulder!
Hem, hem! I see you're not from Boston.
We need good stock in Boston. You're lucky!
meeting me here was providential.
I'm on the side of youth. Hem, hem!

I'll be your guiding lamp in Boston.
Where do you come from?

ROBIN

Deerfield.

MAN IN PERIWIG

Deerfield!
Our bulwark from the savages!
Our martyred village! He's from Deerfield,
Barber. We can use his muscle.

BARBER

You can feel it.

MAN IN PERIWIG

[*Seeing the* BOY]

Look, a child!

BARBER

Shall I shave him?

MAN IN PERIWIG

Yes, shave him.
Shave him and teach him to beat a drum.

BOY

I want a flintlock.

MAN IN PERIWIG

A gun! You scare me!
Come on Apollo, we must march.
We'll put that shoulder to the wheel.
Come, I'll be your host in Boston.

94

My Kinsman, Major Molineux

ROBIN

I have connections here, a kinsman . . .

MAN IN PERIWIG

Of course you have connections here.
They will latch on to you like fleas.
This is your town! Boy! With that leg
You will find kinsmen on the moon.

ROBIN

My kinsman's Major Molineux.

MAN IN PERIWIG

Your kinsman's Major Molineux!
Let go my coat cuff, Fellow. I have
authority, authority!
Hem! Hem! Respect your betters. Your leg
will be acquainted with the stocks
by peep of day! You fellows help me!
Barber, this man's molesting me!

FIRST BARBER

[Closing in]

Don't hit His Honor, Boy!

SECOND BARBER

His Honor
is a lover of mankind!

BOY

Brain him with your cudgel, Robin!

95

ROBIN

Come, Brother, we will see the city;
they're too many of them and one has a razor.

[ROBIN *and the* BOY *back off. Barber shop goes dark*]

BOY

Who was that fellow, Brother Robin?

ROBIN

He is some snotty, county clerk,
chipping and chirping at his betters.
He isn't worth the Major's spit.

BOY

You should have brained him with your stick.

ROBIN

Let's go, now. We must see the city
and try to find our kinsman's house.
I am beginning to think he's out
of town. Look, these men will help us.

[*The tavern lights up. A sign with King George III's head
hangs in front. There's a poster nailed to the door. The* MAN
WITH THE MASK *strolls over and sits in the chair*]

CROWD

Health to the rattlesnake. A health
to Colonel Greenough! He's our man!

MAN WITH MASK

A shine, men, you must shine my shoes
so bright King George will see his face
flash like a guinea on the toe.

CROWD

Health to the rattlesnake!

TAVERN KEEPER

[*Turning to* ROBIN]

You boys
are from the country, I presume.
I envy you, you're seeing Boston
for the first time. Fine town, there's lots
to hold you, English monuments,
docks, houses, and a fleet of tea-ships
begging for buyers. I trust you'll stay;
nobody ever leaves this city.

ROBIN

We come from Deerfield.

TAVERN KEEPER

Then you'll stay;
no Indians scalp us in our beds;
our only scalper is this man here.

[*General laughter*]

ROBIN

Our massacre was eighty years
ago. We're not frontiersmen now,
we've other things to talk about.

BARBER

He has other things to talk about.
This boy's a gentleman. He is
no redskin in a coonskin cap.

ROBIN

I'm on our village council. I've
read Plutarch.

TAVERN KEEPER

You are an ancient Roman.
You'll find you like our commonwealth.
I crave the honor of your custom.
I've whiskey, gin and rum and beer,
and a spruce beer for your brother.

BOY

I want a real beer.

BARBER

Give them beer.

[*Shouting*]

TAVERN KEEPER

Two real beers for the Deerfield boys,
they have the fighting Deerfield spirit.

ROBIN

I'm sure you'll trust me for your money.
I have connections here in Boston,
my kinsman's Major Molineux.
I spent our money on this journey.

MAN

His kinsman's Major Molineux;
sometimes a boy is short of money!

[*Laughter*]

MAN

[Bringing out a silver Liberty Bowl]

    I've something stronger than beer.
Here is the Bowl of Liberty.
The Major dropped this lobster in
the bowl. It spikes the drink.

*[*MAN *puts down his mug and lifts a lobster out of bowl.]*
[Cheers]

ROBIN

   I know
the lobster is a British soldier.

MAN

Yes, there they are.

[The TWO REDCOATS *march on stage as before. Silence. The*
MAN WITH THE MASK *starts writing on a bench. The* SOLDIERS
saunter over to him]

FIRST SOLDIER

What are you writing, Colonel Greenough?

MAN WITH MASK

My will.

FIRST SOLDIER

   Things aren't that desperate.

MAN WITH MASK

I'm adding up my taxes, Redcoat.
Just counting up the figures kills me.
My bankers say I'm burning money.

I can't afford your bed and board
and livery, Soldiers. We'll have to part.

SECOND SOLDIER
I've had enough. We ought to throw
them all in jail.

FIRST SOLDIER
Go easy.

ROBIN

[*Walking shyly up to* SOLDIERS]

Sir,
I need your guidance, I'm looking for
my kinsman, Major Molineux.

FIRST SOLDIER
Watch your words!

SECOND SOLDIER
Damn your insolence!

FIRST SOLDIER
We'll haul you to the Major's court.

[*Shots and screams off stage.* SOLDIERS *leave on the run*]

MAN

[*Pointing to* ROBIN]

He's one of us.

SECOND MAN
He is a spy.

CROWD

Both boys are spies or Tories.

TAVERN KEEPER

[*Drawing* ROBIN *over to the poster*]

Look,
do you see this poster? It says,
"Indentured servant, Jonah Mudge:
ran from his master's house, blue vest,
oak cudgel, leather pants, small brother,
and his master's third best hat.
Pound sterling's offered any man
who nabs and lodges him in jail."
Trudge off, Young Man, you'd better trudge!

CROWD

Trudge, Jonah Mudge, you'd better trudge!

BOY

They're drunk. You'd better hit them, Robin.

ROBIN

They'd only break my stick and brains.

BOY

For God's sake stand and be a man!

ROBIN

No, they're too many, little brother.
Come, I feel like walking.
We haven't seen the city yet.

[*Lights go off.* ROBIN *and* BOY *stand alone*]

BOY

We haven't seen our kinsman, Robin.
I can't see anything.

ROBIN

You'd think
the Major's name would stand us for
a beer. It's a funny thing, Brother, naming
our kinsman, Major Molineux,
sets all these people screaming murder.
Even the soldiers.

[*The house with the bay-window lights up. A woman's red
skirt and bare shoulders are clearly visible through the window.
She is singing*]

WOMAN

Soldiers, sailors.
Whig and Tories, saints and sinners,
I'm your refuge from despair.

ROBIN

[*Knocks*]

Sweet, pretty mistress, help me. I
am tired and lost. I'm looking for
my kinsman, Major Molineux.
You have bright eyes.

WOMAN

I know your kinsman.
Everybody is my kinsman here.

My Kinsman, Major Molineux

ROBIN

Yes, I am sure. You have kind eyes.
My kinsman is a blood relation.

WOMAN

You're my blood relation too then.
What a fine back and leg you have!
You're made right.

ROBIN

       Oh, I will be made
when I find my kinsman. You
must know him, he's a man of some
importance in your city, Lady.

WOMAN

The Major dwells here.

ROBIN

You're thinking of some other major,
Lady; mine is something more
important than a major, he's
a sort of royal governor,
and a man of fortune. Molineux
tea ships sail from here to China.
He has a gilded carriage, twenty
serving men, two flags of England
flying from his lawn. You could hide
your little house behind a sofa
in his drawing-room.

WOMAN

      I know,

your kinsman is a man of parts,
that's why he likes to camp here. Sometimes
his greatness wearies him. These days
even kings draw in their horns,
and mingle with the common people.
Listen, you'll hear him snoring by
the roof.

ROBIN

         I hear a hollow sound.
My kinsman must be happy here.
I envy him this hideaway.

WOMAN

You mean to say you envy him
the mistress of his house. Don't worry,
a kinsman of the Major's is
my kinsman. I knew you right away.
You have your kinsman's leg and shoulders.
He wears an old three-cornered hat
and leather small-clothes here in the rain.
Why, you *are* the good old gentleman,
only you're young! What is this cloth?
You've good material on your leg.

[*The* WOMAN *feels the cloth of* ROBIN's *trousers*]

ROBIN

It's deerskin. I'm from Deerfield, Lady.

WOMAN

You must be starved. I'll make you happy.

My Kinsman, Major Molineux

ROBIN

I'll wait here on your doorstep, Lady.
Run up and tell the Major that
his Deerfield cousins are in town.

WOMAN

The Major'd kill me, if I woke him.
You see, he spilled a little too much
rum in his tea.

ROBIN

I'll leave a note then. I must go,
my little brother needs some sleep.

[WOMAN *takes* ROBIN'S *hat and twirls it on her finger*]

What are you doing with my hat?

WOMAN

I'm showing you our Boston rites
of hospitality. The Major
would kill me, if I turned you out
on such a night. I even have
a downstairs bedroom for your brother.
I find a playroom comes in handy.

BOY

I want to go with Robin.

WOMAN

　　　　Oh, dear,
children keep getting me in trouble.
We have a law.

[*A bell is heard off stage*]

Mother of God!

[*The* WOMAN *ducks into her house*]
[*Her light goes out*]

BOY

Why did the lady slam her door?

ROBIN

The bell reminded her of something.
She has to catch up on her sleep.

BOY

Has the Major left his mansion?
Is he really sleeping here?

ROBIN

How can I tell you? Everyone
answers us in riddles.

BOY

She said,
the Major dwells here.

ROBIN

That's her city
way of being friendly, Brother.

BOY

Robin, the Major could afford
to buy the lady better clothes.
She was almost naked.

ROBIN

        She
was dressed unwisely.

BOY

        Isn't Eve
almost naked in our Bible?

ROBIN

Don't ask so many questions, brother.
I wish I knew the naked truth.

> [*A* WATCHMAN *enters, dishevelled and yawning. He holds a
> lantern with a bell tied to it and a spiked staff*]

WATCHMAN

Stop, we don't allow this sort
of talk about the Bible here.

ROBIN

You are mistaken, Sir. I said
I wished I knew the naked truth.

WATCHMAN

You're in New England. Here we fine
mothers for bearing naked children.
You're leading this child into perdition.
We have a fine for that. What's in
your wallet, Boy?

ROBIN

Nothing.

WATCHMAN

        Nothing! You've been inside then!

ROBIN

Watchman, I'm looking for my kinsman.

WATCHMAN

And you thought you'd find him in this house
Doing his martial drill.

ROBIN

You know him!
My kinsman's Major Molineux.
I see you know him, he will pay you
if you will lead us to his house.

WATCHMAN

[*Singing*]

Your aunt's the lord high sheriff,
your uncle is King George;
if you can't pay the tariff,
the house will let you charge.

ROBIN

I asked for Major Molineux.

WATCHMAN

Keep asking! We are cleaning house.
The Major's lost a lot of money
lately, buying bad real estate.
He can't afford his country cousins.
Move, you filthy, sucking hayseed!
or I'll spike you with my stick!

BOY

Why don't you hit him, brother?

WATCHMAN
　　　　I'll have
you in the stocks by daybreak, Boy.

ROBIN
We'll go, Sir. I'm your countryman
learning the customs of the city.

WATCHMAN

　　[*Goes off singing*]

　　Baggy buttocks, baggy buttocks,
　　The Queen of England's willing
　　To serve you for a shilling
　　And stick you in the stocks.

ROBIN
　　　　We're learning
how to live. The man was drunk.

BOY
Our Deerfield watchmen only drink
at Communion. Something's wrong,
these people need new blood.

ROBIN
　　　　Perhaps
they'll get it. Here's a clergyman,
he'll tell us where to find our kinsman.

　　[*The* CLERGYMAN *comes across the stage. He is awkwardly
　　holding a large English flag on a staff*]

ROBIN

Help me, I beg you, Reverend Sir,
I'm from Deerfield, I'm looking for
my kinsman, Major Molineux.
No one will tell me where he lives.

CLERGYMAN

I have just left the Major's house.
He is my patron and example.
A good man—it's a pity though
he's so outspoken; other good men
misunderstand the Major's meaning.
He just handed me this British
flag to put above my pulpit—
a bit outspoken!

ROBIN

　　　Our country's flag, Sir!

CLERGYMAN

Yes, a bit outspoken. Come
I'll lead you to your kinsman's house.

> [*The* MAN WITH THE MASK *strides hurriedly across the stage,
> and unrolls a rattlesnake flag, which he hands to the* CLERGY-
> MAN, *who has difficulty in managing the two flags*]

MAN WITH MASK

I have a present for you, Parson:
our Rattlesnake. "Don't tread on me!"
it says. I knew you'd want to have one.
Hang it up somewhere in church;

there's nothing like the Rattlesnake
for raising our declining faith.

CLERGYMAN

I thank you, Sir.

MAN WITH MASK

You'd better hurry.
Think of the man who had no garment
for the wedding. Things are moving.

[MAN WITH MASK *hurries off stage*]

CLERGYMAN

[*To himself*]

God help us, if we lose!

[*Turns to go*]

ROBIN

Sir, you're leaving! You promised me
you'd lead me to my kinsman's house.
Please, let me help you with the flags.

CLERGYMAN

I'll see you later. I have to hurry.
I have a sick parishioner,
a whole sick parish! I have a notion
one of these flags will cure us. Which?
Everyone's so emphatic here.
If you should meet your kinsman, tell him
I'm praying for him in my church.

[CLERGYMAN *goes out*]
[*A loud "hem, hem" is heard. The* MAN IN THE PERIWIG *comes*

jauntily forward followed by the TWO BARBERS. *He goes to the house with the bay-window and raps with his cane. The light inside the house goes on. A rattlesnake flag has been nailed to the door. No one sees* ROBIN *and the* BOY]

FIRST BARBER
Look, Your Honor, Mrs. Clark
has taken on the Rattlesnake.

MAN IN PERIWIG
Good, this pricks my fainting courage.
"Don't tread on me!" That's rather odd
for Mrs. Clark.

FIRST BARBER
                    Come on, your Honor.

SECOND BARBER
There's always a first time.

FIRST BARBER
                    Then a second.

MAN IN PERIWIG
Thank God, I've but one life to give
my country.
Lay on, Macduff! I owe this to
my reputation, boys.

FIRST BARBER
                    He owes
his reputation to the boys.

112

SECOND BARBER

Between the devil and the deep
blue sea, Your Honor!

FIRST BARBER

His Honor likes
the sea. Everyone loves a sailor.

MAN IN PERIWIG

Hurry! I'm in torture! Open!
I have authority hem, hem!

> [MAN IN PERIWIG *knocks loudly. The* WOMAN *stands in door-*
> *way*]

WOMAN

> [*Singing*]

> *Where is my boy in leather pants,*
> *who gives a woman what she wants?*

MAN IN PERIWIG

> [*Singing in falsetto*]

> *Woman, I have a royal Crown*
> *your countryman gave the ferryman*
> *a-standing on the strand;*
> *but money goes from hand to hand:*
> *the crown is on the town,*
> *the money's mine, I want to dine.*
> *Whatever we do is our affair,*
> *the breath of freedom's in the air.*

FIRST BARBER

The lady's ballast's in the air.

SECOND BARBER

Two ten pound tea chests. The lady needs
a little uplift from the clergy.

MAN IN PERIWIG

I'm breaking on the foamy breakers!
Help! help!
I wish my lady had a firm,
hard-chested figure like a mast,
but what has love to do with fact?
A lover loves his nemesis;
the patriotic act.

> [*The* MAN IN THE PERIWIG *gives the lady the crown and passes
> in. The lights go out*]

BARBER

Once to every man and nation
comes the time a gentleman
wants to clear his reputation.

TAVERN KEEPER

Once to every man and nation
comes the time a man's a man.

BARBER

His Honor's perished on the blast.

> [*The* BARBER *saunters off along with* TAVERN KEEPER. *The* BOY
> *turns to* ROBIN, *who is lost in thought*]

ROBIN

      I think the Major
has left. By watching I have learned

to read the signs. The Rattlesnake
means Major Molineux is out.
A British flag means he's at home.

BOY

You talk in riddles like the town.

ROBIN

Say what you mean; mean what you say:
that's how we used to talk in Deerfield.
It's not so simple here in the city.

[*The pillared mansion lights up.* ROBIN *and the* BOY *approach
it. The Lion and Unicorn of England are gone. Instead, a
large Rattlesnake flag is showing*]

Brother, we've reached our destination.
This is our kinsman's house. I know it
from the steel engraving that
he gave us when he came to Deerfield.
Our journey's over. Here's our mansion.

BOY

Robin, it has a Rattlesnake.

ROBIN

That means the Major's not at home.

[*The* MAN WITH THE MASK *comes out of the mansion. Half his
face is now fiery red, the other half is still mottled*]

MAN WITH MASK

I am the man on horseback.

ROBIN
         No,
you're walking, Sir.

MAN WITH MASK
         I am a king.

ROBIN
The king's in England. You must be sick.
Have you seen your face? Half's red,
the other half is pocked and mottled.

MAN WITH MASK
Oh I'm as healthy as the times.
I am an image of this city.
Do you see this colored handkerchief?

         [MAN WITH MASK *draws out a small British flag*]

ROBIN
Our British flag, Sir.

MAN WITH / MASK
         Yes, it doesn't
help my illness any more,
when I try to cool my burning brow,
or blow my nose on it.

ROBIN
         I know
a man who used to own this house.
Let's see if he's still here. Perhaps,
my friend can help to heal your sickness.

My Kinsman, Major Molineux

MAN WITH MASK
My face will be entirely red soon;
then I'll be well. Who is your friend?

ROBIN
A kinsman, Major Molineux.

MAN WITH MASK
I have a fellow feeling for him.
The Major used to own this house:
now it's mine. I'm taking over,
I've just signed the final deed.
Do you see my nameplate on the gate?

ROBIN
The Rattlesnake?

MAN WITH MASK
The Rattlesnake.

ROBIN
If I pick up the Rattlesnake,
will it help me find my kinsman?
I think he needs my help. We are
his last relations in the world.

MAN WITH MASK
The last shall be the first, my Boy.

ROBIN
What do you mean? You talk like Christ.

MAN WITH MASK
The first shall be the last, my Boy.

The Major has a heavy hand;
we have been beaten to the ground.

ROBIN

My kinsman has an open hand.

MAN WITH MASK

Ridden like horses, fleeced like sheep,
worked like cattle, clothed and fed
like hounds and hogs!

ROBIN

       I want to find him.

MAN WITH MASK

Whipping-posts, gibbets, bastinadoes
and the rack! I must be moving.

ROBIN

Wait, I'll take up the Rattlesnake.
Please, help me find my kinsman.

[ROBIN *takes hold of the* MAN WITH THE MASK'S *shoulder. The*
MAN *steps back and draws his sword*]

MAN WITH MASK

      Move!
You've torn my cloak. You'd better keep
a civil tongue between your teeth.
I have a mission.

[ROBIN *raises his cudgel. He and the* MAN WITH THE MASK *stand
a moment facing each other*]

BOY

      Brain him, Robin.

Mangle the bastard's bloody face.
He doesn't like our kinsman, Robin.

ROBIN

I only asked for information.

MAN WITH MASK

For information! Information
is my trade. I was a lawyer
before I learned the pleasures of
the military life. The Major
was my first teacher. Now I know you!
I met you at the tavern. You
were short of cash then. Take this crown:
drink to the Major, then a health
to Greenough, and the Rattlesnake.
To Greenough!

ROBIN

You're a fighter.

MAN WITH MASK

I hate war, wars leave us where
they find us, don't they, boy
Let's talk about my health.

ROBIN

Where can
I find my kinsman?

MAN WITH MASK

He owned this house.
Men used to find him here all day,

before the storms disturbed his judgment,
He's out now ranging through the town,
looking for new accommodations.
Wait here. You'll meet him on his walk.

> [*Strides off singing*]

> *The king is in his counting house;*
> *we're counting up his money.*

BOY
Why was that fellow's face half red now?
He's changing color.

ROBIN
       I don't know.
He is someone out of "Revelations"—
Hell revolting on its jailers.

> [*The church lights up a little.* ROBIN *walks over to it, and looks in a window*]

Our church is empty, brother. Moonbeams
are trembling on the snow-pure pews,
the altar's drowned in radiant fog,
a single restless ray has crept
across the open Bible.

> [*Turns to a gravestone by the church*]

       I'm lonely.
What's this? A gravestone? A grave? Whose grave?
I think the Major must have died:
everything tells me he is gone
and nothing is forever.

[*Turns back to the church*]

Brother,
the moon's the only worshipper!

[*The* CLERGYMAN *comes out of the church. He lays a white clay pipe on the steps and holds up a little colored celluloid whirligig*]

CLERGYMAN

The wind has died.

ROBIN

What are you doing?

CLERGYMAN

I'm playing with this whirligig,
and waiting to see which way the wind
will veer. It's quite amusing, Son,
trying to guess the whims of the wind.
I am waiting for a sign.
A strange thing for a modern churchman.

ROBIN

My father says the Church is a rock.

CLERGYMAN

Yes, yes, a rock is blind. That's why
I've shut my eyes.

ROBIN

I see my father. He's the Deerfield
minister, and Church of England.
You remind me of my father.

CLERGYMAN

Be careful, son. Call no man father:
that's what we tell the Roman clergy;
sometimes I think we go too far,
they get their people out for Mass.

ROBIN

Father. When I shut
my eyes, I dream I'm back in Deerfield.
The people sit in rows below
the old oak; a horseman stops to water
his horse and to refresh his soul.
I hear my father holding forth
thanksgiving, hope and all the mercies—

CLERGYMAN

     Those village
pastors! Once they used to preach
as if the world were everlasting;
each Sunday was longer than a summer!
That's gone now. We have competition:
taverns, papers, politics
and trade. It takes a wolfhound now
to catch a flock!

ROBIN

     Why are you waiting
for the wind?

CLERGYMAN

  [*Taking up two little flags*]
    Do you see

these two flags? One's the Union Jack,
the other is the Rattlesnake.
The wind will tell me which to fly.

ROBIN

I'm thinking of the absent one.
My kinsman, Major Molineux
is absent. The storms have hurt his house
lately. No one will help me find him.

CLERGYMAN

Perhaps the wind will blow him back.

ROBIN

I met a strange man, Colonel Greenough;
Half of his face was red, and half
was pocked. He said, "Wait here, and you
will meet your kinsman on his walk."

CLERGYMAN

You'd better wait here then. That red
and pocked man tends to speak the truth.

ROBIN

Why was his face two-colors, Father?

CLERGYMAN

He is an image of the city.
If his whole face turns red as blood,
We'll have to fly the Rattlesnake.

ROBIN

Say more about my kinsman, Father.
You said he was your friend and patron.

CLERGYMAN

Poor Molineux! he served the clergy
somewhat better than this city.
He had a special pew, you know.
He used to set a grand example.

ROBIN

He used to! You speak as if he were dead!

CLERGYMAN

Men blamed me, but I liked to watch
his red coat blazing like the sunset
at Sunday morning service here.
He was an easy-going fellow,
a lover of life, no Puritan.
He had invention, used to send
two six foot Privates here to help
with the collection. Yes, I had
to like him. He had his flaws, of course.

ROBIN

A red coat blazing like the sunrise,
that's how the Major was in Deerfield;
the gold lion of England shone
on his gilded carriage. He had a little
white scar like a question mark
on his right cheek. He got it killing
Frenchmen. He seemed to hold the world
like a gold ball in the palm of his hand.
Ours for the asking! All! We are
his last relations in the world!

CLERGYMAN

No one will dispute your claim.

ROBIN

The Major said he was the King's
intelligence in Massachusetts.

CLERGYMAN

No one will dispute his claim.
What shall we do with people? They
get worse and worse, but God improves.
God was green in Moses' time;
little by little though, he blossomed.
First came the prophets, then our Lord,
and then the Church.

ROBIN

        The Church?

CLERGYMAN

                  The Church
gets more enlightened every day.
We've learned to disregard the Law
and look at persons. Who is my neighbor?
Anyone human is my neighbor. Sometimes
my neighbor is a man from Sodom.

> [*Great noise of shouting.* ALL FORMER CHARACTERS, *except the*
> MAN WITH THE MASK, *parade across the stage.* MOST OF THEM
> *wave Rattlesnake flags*]

ROBIN

Father, I see two clergymen,
they're waving flags.

CLERGYMAN

I see my sign.

[*Snaps the whirligig with his thumb*]

Look, the wind has risen! Wherever
the spirit calls me, I must follow.

CROWD

Hurrah for the Republic!
Down with Major Molineux!

[*The* PEOPLE *sing a verse of Yankee Doodle, and draw* COLONEL
GREENOUGH *on stage in a red, white and blue cart. He stands
up and draws his sword. One can see that his face is now entirely red*]

MAN WITH MASK

The die is cast! I say, the die is cast.

ROBIN

Look at the Colonel,
his whole face is red as blood!

MAN WITH MASK

Major Molineux is coming.

CLERGYMAN

Are you sure we're strong enough?

MAN WITH MASK

Every British soldier in Boston
is killed or captured.

CROWD

Don't tread on me!
Don't tread on me! Don't tread on me!

ROBIN

What can I do to help my kinsman?

CLERGYMAN

Swap your flag and save your soul.

ROBIN

I want to save my kinsman, Father.

CLERGYMAN

No, no, Son, do as I do. Here, hold
this flag a moment, while I speak.

> [*The* CLERGYMAN *hands* ROBIN *his Rattlesnake flag, tosses away
> the whirligig, breaks his clay pipe, then takes a chair and
> stands on it while he addresses the* CROWD *with both hands
> raised. Throughout the crowd scene,* ROBIN *stands uncon-
> sciously holding the flag and suffering*]

How long, how long now, Men of Boston!
You've faced the furious tyrant's trident,
you've borne the blandishments of Sodom.
The Day of Judgment is at hand,
now we'll strip the scarlet whore,
King George shall swim in scarlet blood,
Now Nebuchadnezzar shall eat grass and die.
How long! How long! O Men of Boston,
behave like men, if you are men!

> [*The* PEOPLE *cheer and take the* CLERGYMAN *on their shoulders*]

You've drawn the sword, Boys, throw away
the scabbard!

[*The* CLERGYMAN *draws a sword and throws down the scab-bard. Many of the* PEOPLE, *including the* PROSTITUTE, *draw swords and throw the scabbards rattling across the stage. They draw* MAJOR MOLINEUX *on stage in a red cart. He is partly tarred and feathered; one cheek is bleeding; his red British uniform is torn; he shakes with terror*]

ROBIN

Oh my kinsman, my dear kinsman,
they have wounded you!

MAN WITH MASK

Throw the boy from Deerfield out,
he has no garment for our wedding.

CLERGYMAN

No, let him stay, he is just a boy.

[ROBIN, *unthinking, holds the flag in front of him, while his eyes are fixed in horror and pity on the figure of the Major. The* BOY, *unconsciously, too, mingles among the* CROWD *without thinking. Someone asks him to give some dirt to throw at the* MAJOR *and he unthinkingly picks up some from a basket, and hands it to the* TAVERN KEEPER, *who throws it at the* MAJOR]

ROBIN

[*With a loud cry, but unconsciously waving the flag in his grief*]

Oh my poor kinsman, you are hurt!

CROWD

Don't tread on me! Don't tread on me!

My Kinsman, Major Molineux

[*The* MAJOR *slowly staggers to his feet. Slowly he stretches out his right arm and points to* ROBIN]

MAJOR MOLINEUX

Et tu, Brute!

TAVERN KEEPER

The Major wants to teach us Latin.

[*The* CROWD *laughs, and* ROBIN, *once more without thinking, laughs too, very loudly*]
[TAVERN KEEPER *goes up to the* MAJOR *and hands him a Rattlesnake flag*]

You're out of step, Sir. Here's your flag.

[*The* MAJOR *lurches a few steps from the cart, grinds the Rattlesnake underfoot, then turns and addresses the crowd*]

MAJOR MOLINEUX

Long live King George! Long live King George!
I'll sing until you cut my tongue out!

CROWD

Throw the Major in the river,
in the river, in the river!

[*With a grating sound, the* FERRYMAN *appears at the side of the stage, pushing the prow of his dory. The* MAJOR *staggers towards the* FERRYMAN]

MAJOR MOLINEUX

[*To* FERRYMAN]

Help me in my trouble. Let
me cross the river to my King!

[*The* FERRYMAN *stiffens.* THE MAN WITH THE MASK *throws him a silver crown*]

MAN WITH MASK

Ferryman, here's a silver crown,
take him or leave him, we don't care.

FERRYMAN

    [*Still more threatening*]

The crown's no longer currency.

    [*The* FERRYMAN *kicks the crown into the water*]

MAJOR MOLINEUX

Boatman, you rowed me here in state;
save me, now that I'm fallen!

FERRYMAN

There's no returning on my boat.

MAJOR MOLINEUX

    [*Stretching out his hands and grappling the* FERRYMAN]

Save me in the name of God!

    [*The* FERRYMAN *pushes the* MAJOR *off and hits him on the
head with his oar. The* MAJOR *screams, and lies still*]

FERRYMAN

He's crossed the river into his kingdom;
all tyrants must die as this man died.

    [*One by one, the* PRINCIPAL CHARACTERS *come up and look at
the* MAJOR]

CLERGYMAN

He's dead. He had no time to pray.
I wish he'd called me. O Lord, remember

his past kindness to the Church;
all tyrants must die as this man died.

MAN IN PERIWIG

[*Taking the* MAJOR'S *empty scabbard*]

I have the Major's sword of office;
hem, hem, I have authority.

FIRST BARBER

His Honor has the hollow scabbard.

MAN IN PERIWIG

They build men right in England. Take him
all in all, he was a man;
all tyrants must die as this man died.

TAVERN KEEPER

[*Holding a poster*]

Look, this poster says the town
of Boston offers a thousand guineas
to anyone who kills the Major.
I'll take his wallet for the cause.
All tyrants must die as this man died.

PROSTITUTE

[*Taking the* MAJOR'S *hat*]

I'll need this hat to hide my head.
They build men right in England. Take him
all in all, he was a man;
all tyrants must die as this man died.

MAN WITH MASK

[*Plunging his sword in the* MAJOR]

Sic semper tyrannis!

FERRYMAN

His fare is paid now;
the Major's free to cross the river.

[*The* FERRYMAN *loads* MAJOR MOLINEUX's *body on his boat,
and pushes off*]

CLERGYMAN

[*Coming up to* MAN WITH MASK]

Your hand! I want
to shake your hand, Sir. A great day!

MAN WITH MASK

Great and terrible! There's nothing
I can do about it now.

[*Turns to* ROBIN]

Here, boy, here's the Major's sword;
perhaps, you'll want a souvenir.

[CROWD *starts to leave.* ROBIN *and* BOY *alone*]

BOY

The Major's gone. We'll have to go
Back home. There's no one here to help us.

ROBIN

Yes, Major Molineux is dead.

[*Starts sadly towards the river*]

132

CROWD

Long live the Republic! Long live the Republic!

BOY

Look, Robin, I have found a flintlock.

> [ROBIN *looks wistfully at the* CROWD, *now almost entirely gone.*
> *He pauses and then answers in a daze*]

ROBIN

A flintlock?

BOY

Well, that's all I came to Boston for, I guess.
Let's go, I see the ferryman.

ROBIN

> [*Still inattentive*]

I'm going.

> [ROBIN *takes his brother's hand and turns firmly towards the*
> *city*]

BOY

We are returning to the city!

> [ALL THE PEOPLE *are gone now, the lights start to go out. A*
> *red sun shows on the river*]

ROBIN

Yes, brother, we are staying here.
Look, the lights are going out,
the red sun's moving on the river.
Where will it take us to? . . . It's strange
to be here on our own—and free.

BOY

[Sighting along his flintlock]

Major Molineux is dead.

ROBIN

Yes, Major Molineux is dead.

CURTAIN

BENITO CERENO

ORIGINAL CAST FOR
Benito Cereno
Premiere November 1, 1964

Captain Amasa Delano: LESTER RAWLINS
John Perkins: JACK RYLAND
Don Benito Cereno: FRANK LANGELLA
Babu: ROSCOE LEE BROWNE
Atufal: CLAYTON CORBIN
Francesco: MICHAEL SCHULTZ
American Sailors: CONWAY W. YOUNG, ROBERT TINSLEY,
    RICHARD KJELLAND, E. EMMET WALSCH,
    HOWARD MARTIN
Spanish Sailors: LUKE ANDREAS, WILLIAM JACOBSON,
    JAMES ZAFERES
Negro Slaves: WOODIE KING, LONNIE STEVENS,
    GEORGE A. SHARPE, HURMAN FITZGERALD,
    ERNEST BAXTER, ASTON YOUNG, JUNE BROWN,
    MARY FOREMAN, GENE FOREMAN, JUDITH BYRD,
    M. S. MITCHELL, LANE FLOYD, PAUL PLUMMER,
    WALTER JONES, ETHAN COURTNEY

The scene

About the year 1800, an American sealing vessel, the *President Adams,* at anchor in an island harbor off the coast of Trinidad. The stage is part of the ship's deck. Everything is unnaturally clean, bare and ship-shape. To one side, a polished, coal-black cannon. The American captain, AMASA DELANO from Duxbury, Massachusetts, sits in a cane chair. He is a strong, comfortable looking man in his early thirties who wears a spotless blue coat and white trousers. Incongruously, he has on a straw hat and smokes a corncob pipe. Beside him stands JOHN PERKINS, his bosun, a very stiff, green young man, a relative of DELANO'S. THREE SAILORS, one carrying an American flag, enter. EVERYONE stands at attention and salutes with machinelike exactitude. Then the THREE SAILORS march off-stage. DELANO and PERKINS are alone.

DELANO

There goes the most beautiful woman in South America.

PERKINS

We never see any women, Sir;
just this smothering, overcast Equator,
a seal or two,
the flat dull sea,
and a sky like a gray wasp's nest.

DELANO

I wasn't talking about women,
I was calling your attention to the American flag.

PERKINS

Yes, Sir! I wish we were home in Duxbury.

DELANO

We are home. America is wherever her flag flies.
My own deck is the only place in the world
where I feel at home.

PERKINS

That's too much for me, Captain Delano.
I mean I wish I were at home with my wife;
these world cruises are only for bachelors.

DELANO

Your wife will keep. You should smoke, Perkins.
Smoking turns men into philosophers
and swabs away their worries.
I can see my wife and children or not see them
in each puff of blue smoke.

PERKINS

You are always tempting me, Sir!
I try to keep fit,
I want to return to my wife as fit as I left her.

DELANO

You're much too nervous, Perkins.
Travel will shake you up. You should let
a little foreign dirt rub off on you.

I've taught myself to speak Spanish like a Spaniard.
At each South American port, they mistake me for a
Castilian Don.

PERKINS

Aren't you lowering yourself a little, Captain?
Excuse me, Sir, I have been wanting to ask you a question.
Don't you think our President, Mr. Jefferson, is
        lowering himself
by being so close to the French?
I'd feel a lot safer in this unprotected place
if we'd elected Mr. Adams instead of Mr. Jefferson.

DELANO

The better man ran second!
Come to think of it, he rather let us down
by losing the election just after we had named this ship,
the *President Adams*. Adams is a nervous dry fellow.
When you've travelled as much as I have,
you'll learn that that sort doesn't export, Perkins.
Adams didn't get a vote outside New England!

PERKINS

He carried every New England state;
that was better than winning the election.
I'm afraid I'm a dry fellow, too, Sir.

DELANO

Not when I've educated you!
When I am through with you, Perkins,
you'll be as worldly as the Prince Regent of England,
only you'll be a first class American officer.

I'm all for Jefferson, he has the popular touch.
Of course he's read too many books,
but I've always said an idea or two won't sink
        our Republic.
I'll tell you this, Perkins,
Mr. Jefferson is a gentleman and an American.

PERKINS

They say he has two illegitimate Negro children.

DELANO

The more the better! That's the quickest way
to raise the blacks to our level.
I'm surprised you swallow such Federalist bilge, Perkins!
I told you Mr. Jefferson is a gentleman and an American;
when a man's in office, Sir, we all pull behind him!

PERKINS

Thank God our Revolution ended where the French
        one began.

DELANO

Oh the French! They're like the rest of the Latins,
they're hardly white people,
they start with a paper republic
and end with a toy soldier, like Bonaparte.

PERKINS

Yes, Sir. I see a strange sail making for the harbor.
They don't know how to sail her.

DELANO

Hand me my telescope.

PERKINS

Aye, aye, Sir!

DELANO

[*With telescope*]

I see an ocean undulating in long scoops of swells;
it's set like the beheaded French Queen's high wig;
the sleek surface is like waved lead,
cooled and pressed in the smelter's mould.
I see flights of hurried gray fowl,
patches of fluffy fog.
They skim low and fitfully above the decks,
like swallows sabering flies before a storm.
This gray boat foreshadows something wrong.

PERKINS

It does, Sir!
They don't know how to sail her!

DELANO

I see a sulphurous haze above her cabin,
the new sun hangs like a silver dollar to her stern;
low creeping clouds blow on from them to us.

PERKINS

What else, Sir?

DELANO

The yards are woolly
the ship is furred with fog.
On the cracked and rotten head-boards,
the tarnished, gilded letters say, the *San Domingo*.

A rat's-nest messing up the deck,
black faces in white sheets are fussing with the ropes.
I think it's a cargo of Dominican monks.

PERKINS

Dominican monks, Sir! God help us,
I thought they were outlawed in the new world.

DELANO

No, it's nothing. I see they're only slaves.
The boat's transporting slaves.

PERKINS

Do you believe in slavery, Captain Delano?

DELANO

In a civilized country, Perkins,
everyone disbelieves in slavery,
everyone disbelieves in slavery and wants slaves.
We have the perfect uneasy answer;
in the North, we don't have them and want them;
Mr. Jefferson has them and fears them.

PERKINS

Is that how you answer, Sir,
when a little foreign dirt has rubbed off on you?

DELANO

Don't ask me such intense questions.
You should take up smoking, Perkins.
There was a beautiful, dumb English actress—
I saw her myself once in London.
They wanted her to look profound,

so she read Plato and the Bible and Benjamin Franklin,
and thought about them every minute.
She still looked like a moron.
Then they told her to think about nothing.
She thought about nothing, and looked like Socrates.
That's smoking, Perkins, you think about nothing and
     look deep.

PERKINS

I don't believe in slavery, Sir.

DELANO

You don't believe in slavery or Spaniards
or smoking or long cruises or monks or Mr. Jefferson!
You are a Puritan, all faith and fire.

PERKINS

Yes, Sir.

DELANO

God save America from Americans!

[*Takes up the telescope*]

I see octogonal network bagging out
from her heavy top like decayed beehives.
The battered forecastle looks like a raped Versailles.
On the stern-piece, I see the fading arms of Spain.
There's a masked satyr, or something
with its foot on a big white goddess.
She has quite a figure.

PERKINS

They oughtn't to be allowed on the ocean!

DELANO

Who oughtn't? Goddesses?

PERKINS

I mean Spaniards, who cannot handle a ship,
and mess up its hull with immoral statues.

DELANO

You're out of step. You're much too dry.
Bring me my three-cornered hat.
Order some men to clear a whaleboat.
I am going to bring water and fresh fish to the
    San Domingo.
These people have had some misfortune, Perkins!

PERKINS

Aye, aye, Sir.

DELANO

Spaniards? The name gets you down,
you think their sultry faces and language
make them Zulus.
You take the name *Delano*—
I've always thought it had some saving
Italian or Spanish virtue in it.

PERKINS

Yes, Sir.

DELANO

A Spaniard isn't a negro under the skin,
particularly a Spaniard from Spain—
these South American ones mix too much with the Indians.

146

Once you get inside a Spaniard,
he talks about as well as your wife in Duxbury.

PERKINS

[*Shouting*]

A boat for the captain! A whaleboat for Captain Delano!

[*A bosun's whistle is heard, the lights dim. When they come up, we are on the deck of the* San Domingo, *the same set, identical except for litter and disorder.* THREE AMERICAN SAIL-ORS *climb on board. They are followed by* PERKINS *and* DELANO, *now wearing a three-cornered hat. Once on board, the* AMER-ICAN SAILORS *salute* DELANO *and stand stiffly at attention like toys.* NEGROES *from the* San Domingo *drift silently and furtively forward*]

DELANO

I see a wen of barnacles hanging to the waterline of
    this ship.
It sticks out like the belly of a pregnant woman.
Have a look at our dory Bosun.

PERKINS

Aye, aye, Sir!

[*By now, about twenty blacks and two Spanish sailors have drifted in. They look like some gaudy, shabby, unnautical charade, and pay no attention to the Americans, until an unseen figure in the rigging calls out a single sharp warning in an unknown tongue. Then they all rush forward, shouting, waving their arms and making inarticulate cries like birds. Three shrill warnings come from the rigging. Dead silence. The men from the* SAN DOMINGO *press back in a dense semicircle. One by one, individuals come forward, make showy bows to* DELANO, *and speak*]

147

FIRST NEGRO

Scurvy, Master Yankee!

SECOND NEGRO

Yellow fever, Master Yankee!

THIRD NEGRO

Two men knocked overboard rounding Cape Horn,
Master Yankee!

FOURTH NEGRO

Nothing to eat, Master Yankee!

NEGRO WOMAN

Nothing to drink, Master Yankee!

SECOND NEGRO WOMAN

Our mouths are dead wood, Master Yankee!

DELANO

You see, Perkins,
these people have had some misfortune.

> [*General hubbub, muttering, shouts, gestures, ritual and
> dumbshow of distress. The rigging, hitherto dark, lightens,
> as the sun comes out of a cloud, and shows* THREE OLD NE-
> GROES, *identical down to their shabby patches. They perch
> on cat's-heads; their heads are grizzled like dying willow tops;
> each is picking bits of unstranded rope for oakum. It is they
> who have been giving the warnings that control the people
> below. Everyone,* DELANO *along with the rest, looks up.* DELANO
> *turns aside and speaks to* PERKINS]

It is like a Turkish bazaar.

PERKINS

They are like gypsies showing themselves for money
at a county fair, Sir.

DELANO

This is enchanting after the blank gray roll of the ocean!
Go tell the Spanish captain I am waiting for him.

[PERKINS *goes off. Sharp warnings from the* OAKUM-PICKERS.
*A big black spread of canvas is pulled creakingly and cere-
moniously aside.* SIX FIGURES *stand huddled on a platform
about four feet from the deck. They look like weak old invalids in bathrobes and nightcaps until they strip to the waist
and turn out to be huge, shining young negroes. Saying nothing, they set to work cleaning piles of rusted hatchets. From
time to time, they turn and clash their hatchets together with
a rhythmic shout.* PERKINS *returns*]

PERKINS

Their captain's name is Don Benito Cereno,
he sends you his compliments, Sir.
He looks more like a Mexican planter than a seaman.
He's put his fortune on his back:
he doesn't look as if he had washed since they left port.

DELANO

Did you tell him I was waiting for him?
A captain should be welcomed by his fellow-captain.
I can't understand this discourtesy.

PERKINS

He's coming, but there's something wrong with him.

[BENITO CERENO, *led by his negro servant,* BABU, *enters.* BENITO,

*looking sick and dazed, is wearing a sombrero and is dressed
with a singular but shabby richness. Head bent to one side,
he leans in a stately coma against the rail, and stares unsee-
ingly at* DELANO. BABU, *all in scarlet, and small and quick,
keeps whispering, pointing and pulling at* BENITO'S *sleeve.*
DELANO *walks over to them*]

DELANO

Your hand, Sir. I am Amasa Delano,
captain of the *President Adams,*
a sealing ship from the United States.
This is your lucky day,
the sun is out of hiding for the first time in two weeks,
and here I am aboard your ship
like the Good Samaritan with fresh food and water.

BENITO

The Good Samaritan? Yes, yes,
we mustn't use the Scriptures lightly.
Welcome, Captain. It is the end of the day.

DELANO

The end? It's only morning.
I loaded and lowered a whaleboat
as soon as I saw how awkwardly your ship was making for
    the harbor.

BENITO

Your whaleboat's welcome, Captain.
I am afraid I am still stunned by the storm.

DELANO

Buck up. Each day is a new beginning.
Assign some sailors to help me dole out my provisions.

BENITO

I have no sailors.

BABU

[*In a quick sing-song:*]

Scurvy, yellow fever,
ten men knocked off on the Horn,
doldrums, nothing to eat, nothing to drink!
By feeding us, you are feeding the King of Spain.

DELANO

Sir, your slave has a pretty way of talking.
What do you need?

[DELANO *waits for* BENITO *to speak. When nothing more is said, he shifts awkwardly from foot to foot, then turns to his* SAILORS]

Stand to, men!

[*The* AMERICAN SAILORS, *who have been lounging and gaping, stand in a row, as if a button had been pressed*]

Lay our fish and water by the cabin!

[*The* SAILORS *arrange the watercans and baskets of fish by the cabin. A sharp whistle comes from the* OAKUM-PICKERS. *Almost instantly, the provisions disappear*]

Captain Cereno, you are surely going to taste my water!

BENITO

A captain is a servant, almost a slave, Sir.

DELANO

No, a captain's a captain.

I am sending for more provisions.
Stand to!

[*The* AMERICAN SAILORS *stand to*]

Row back to the ship. When you get there,
take on five hogsheads of fresh water,
and fifty pounds of soft bread.

[FIRST SAILOR *salutes and goes down the ladder*]

Bring all our remaining pumpkins!

[SECOND *and* THIRD SAILORS *salute and go down the ladder*]

My bosun and I will stay on board,
until our boat returns.
I imagine you can use us.

BENITO

Are you going to stay here alone?
Won't your ship be lost without you?
Won't you be lost without your ship?

BABU

Listen to Master!
He is the incarnation of courtesy, Yankee Captain.
Your ship doesn't need you as much as we do.

DELANO

Oh, I've trained my crew.
I can sail my ship in my sleep.

[*Leaning over the railing and calling*]

Men, bring me a box of lump sugar,
and six bottles of my best cider.

[*Turning to* BENITO]

Cider isn't my favorite drink, Don Benito,
but it's a New England specialty;
I'm ordering six bottles for your table.

[BABU *whispers and gestures to* DON BENITO, *who is exhausted
and silent*]

BABU

Une bouteille du vin [*to* NEGROES]
My master wishes to give you a bottle
of the oldest wine in Seville.

[*He whistles. A negro woman rushes into the cabin and returns with a dusty beribboned bottle, which she holds like
a baby*]
[BABU *ties a rope around the bottle*]

BABU

I am sending this bottle of wine to your cabin.
When you drink it, you will remember us.
Do you see these ribbons? The crown of Spain is tied
      to one.
Forgive me for tying a rope around the King of
      Spain's neck.

[*Lowers the wine on the rope to the whaleboat*]

DELANO

[*Shouting to his* SAILORS]

Pick up your oars!

SAILORS

Aye, aye, Sir!

DELANO

We're New England Federalists;
we can drink the King of Spain's health.

[BENITO *stumbles off-stage on* BABU'S *arm*]

PERKINS

Captain Cereno hasn't travelled as much as you have;
I don't think he knew what you meant by the New England
Federalists.

DELANO

[*Leaning comfortably on the rail; half to himself and half to*
PERKINS]

The wind is dead. We drift away.
We will be left alone all day,
here in this absentee empire.
Thank God, I know my Spanish!

PERKINS

You'll have to watch them, Sir.
Brown men in charge of black men—
it doesn't add up to much!
This Babu, I don't trust him!
Why doesn't he talk with a Southern accent,
Like Mr. Jefferson? They're out of hand, Sir!

DELANO

Nothing relaxes order more than misery.
They need severe superior officers.
They haven't one.

Now, if this Benito were a man of energy . . .
a Yankee . . .

PERKINS

How can a Spaniard sail?

DELANO

Some can. There was Vasco da Gama and Columbus . . .
No, I guess they were Italians. Some can,
but this captain is tubercular.

PERKINS

Spaniards and Negroes have no business on a ship.

DELANO

Why is this captain so indifferent to me?
If only I could stomach his foreign reserve!
This absolute dictator of his ship
only gives orders through his slaves!
He is like some Jesuit-haunted Hapsburg king
about to leave the world and hope the world will end.

PERKINS

He said he was lost in the storm.

DELANO

Perhaps it's only policy,
a captain's icy dignity
obliterating all democracy—

PERKINS

He's like someone walking in his sleep.

DELANO

Ah, slumbering dominion!
He is so self-conscious in his imbecility . . .
No, he's sick. He sees his men no more than me.
This ship is like a crowded immigration boat;
it needs severe superior officers,
the friendly arm of a strong mate.
Perhaps, I ought to take it over by force.
No, they're sick, they've been through the plague.
I'll go and speak and comfort my fellow captain.
I think you can help me, Captain. I'm feeling useless.
My own thoughts oppress me, there's so much to do.
I wonder if you would tell me the whole sad story of
        your voyage.
Talk to me as captain to captain.
We have sailed the same waters.
Please tell me your story.

BENITO

A story? A story! That's out of place.
When I was a child, I used to beg for stories back in Lima.
Now my tongue's tied and my heart is bleeding.

> [*Stops talking, as if his breath were gone. He stares for a few
> moments, then looks up at the rigging, as if he were counting
> the ropes one by one.* DELANO *turns abruptly to* PERKINS]

DELANO

Go through the ship, Perkins,
and see if you can find me a Spaniard who can talk.

BENITO

You must be patient, Captain Delano;

if we only see with our eyes,
sometimes we cannot see at all.

DELANO

I stand corrected, Captain;
tell me about your voyage.

BENITO

It's now a hundred and ninety days . . .
This ship, well manned, well officered, with several
      cabin passengers,
carrying a cargo of Paraguay tea and Spanish cutlery.
That parcel of Negro slaves, less than four score now,
was once three hundred souls.
Ten sailors and three officers fell from the mainyard off
      the Horn;
part of our rigging fell overboard with them,
as they were beating down the icy sail.
We threw away all our cargo,
Broke our waterpipes,
Lashed them on deck
this was the chief cause of our suffering.

DELANO

I must interrupt you, Captain.
How did you happen to have three officers on
      the mainyard?
I never heard of such a disposal,
it goes against all seamanship.

BABU

Our officers never spared themselves;

if there was any danger, they rushed in
to save us without thinking.

DELANO

I can't understand such an oversight.

BABU

There was no oversight. My master had a hundred eyes.
He had an eye for everything.
Sometimes the world falls on a man.
The sea wouldn't let Master act like a master,
yet he saved himself and many lives.
He is still a rich man, and he saved the ship.

BENITO

Oh my God, I wish the world had fallen on me,
and the terrible cold sea had drowned me;
that would have been better than living through what I've
lived through!

BABU

He is a good man, but his mind is off;
he's thinking about the fever when the wind stopped—
poor, poor Master!
Be patient, Yankee Captain, these fits are short,
Master will be the master once again.

BENITO

The scurvy was raging through us.
We were on the Pacific. We were invalids
and couldn't man our mangled spars.
A hurricane blew us northeast through the fog.
Then the wind died.

We lay in irons fourteen days in unknown waters,
our black tongues stuck through our mouths,
but we couldn't mend our broken waterpipes.

BABU

Always those waterpipes,
he dreams about them like a pile of snakes!

BENITO

Yellow fever followed the scurvy,
the long heat thickened in the calm,
my Spaniards turned black and died like slaves,
The blacks died too. I am my only officer left.

BABU

Poor, poor Master! He had a hundred eyes,
he lived our lives for us.
He is still a rich man.

BENITO

In the smart winds beating us northward,
our torn sails dropped like sinkers in the sea;
each day we dropped more bodies.
Almost without a crew, canvas, water, or a wind,
we were bounced about by the opposing waves
through cross-currents and the weedy calms,
and dropped our dead.
Often we doubled and redoubled on our track
like children lost in jungle. The thick fog
hid the Continent and our only port from us.

BABU

We were poor kidnapped jungle creatures.

We only lived on what he could give us.
He had a hundred eyes, he was the master.

These Negroes saved me, Captain.
Through the long calamity,
they were as gentle as their owner, Don Aranda, promised.
Don Aranda took away their chains before he died.

BABU

Don Aranda saved our lives, but we couldn't save his.
Even in Africa I was a slave.
He took away my chains.

BENITO

I gave them the freedom of my ship.
I did not think they were crates or cargo or cannibals.
But it was Babu—under God, I swear I owe my life
        to Babu!
He calmed his ignorant, wild brothers,
never left me, saved the *San Domingo*.

BABU

Poor, poor Master. He is still a rich man.
Don't speak of Babu. Babu is the dirt under your feet.
He did his best.

DELANO

You are a good fellow, Babu.
You are the salt of the earth. I envy you, Don Benito;
he is no slave, Sir, but your friend.

160

BENITO

Yes, he is salt in my wounds.
I can never repay him, I mean.
Excuse me, Captain, my strength is gone.
I have done too much talking. I want to rest.

[BABU *leads* BENITO *to a shabby straw chair at the side.* BENITO *sits.* BABU *fans him with his sombrero*]

PERKINS

He's a fine gentleman, but no seaman.
A cabin boy would have known better
than to send his three officers on the mainyard.

DELANO

[*Paying no attention*]

A terrible story. I would have been unhinged myself.

[*Looking over toward* BABU *and* BENITO]

There's a true servant. They do things better
in the South and in South America—
trust in return for trust!
The beauty of that relationship is unknown
in New England. We're too much alone
in Massachusetts, Perkins.
How do our captains and our merchants live,
each a republic to himself.
Even Sam Adams had no friends and only loved the mob.

PERKINS

Sir, you are forgetting that
New England seamanship brought them their slaves.

Oh, just our Southern slaves;
we had nothing to do with these fellows.

PERKINS

The ocean would be a different place
if every Spaniard served an apprenticeship on an
    American ship
before he got his captain's papers.

DELANO

This captain's a gentleman, not a sailor.
His little yellow hands
got their command before they held a rope—
in by the cabin-window, not the hawse-hole!
Do you want to know why
they drifted hog-tied in those easy calms—
inexperience, sickness, impotence and aristocracy!

PERKINS

Here comes Robinson Crusoe and his good man Friday.

DELANO

We don't beat a man when he's down.

[BENITO *advances uncertainly on* BABU'S *arm*]

I am glad to see you on your feet again,
That's the only place for a Captain, sir!
I have the cure for you, I have decided
to bring you medicine and a sufficient supply of water.
A first class deck officer, a man from Salem,
shall be stationed on your quarter deck,

a temporary present from my owners.
We shall refit your ship and clear this mess.

BENITO

You will have to clear away the dead.

BABU

This excitement is bad for him, Yankee Master.
He's lived with death. He lives on death still;
this sudden joy will kill him. You've heard
how thirsty men die from overdrinking!
His heart is with his friend, our owner, Don Aranda.

BENITO

I am the only owner.

> [*He looks confused and shaken*]
> [BABU *scurries off and brings up the straw chair.* BENITO *sits*]

DELANO

Your friend is dead? He died of fever?

BENITO

He died very slowly and in torture.
He was the finest man in Lima.
We were brought up together,
I am lost here.

DELANO

Pardon me, Sir. You are young at sea.
My experience tells me what your trouble is:
this is the first body you have buried in the ocean.
I had a friend like yours, a warm honest fellow,
who would look you in the eye—

we had to throw him to the sharks.
Since then I've brought embalming gear on board.
Each man of mine shall have a Christian grave on land.
You wouldn't shake so, if Don Aranda were on board,
I mean, if you'd preserved the body.

BENITO

If he were on board this ship?
If I had preserved his body?

BABU

Be patient, Master!
We still have the figurehead.

DELANO

You have the figurehead?

BABU

You see that thing wrapped up in black cloth?
It's a figurehead Don Aranda bought us in Spain.
It was hurt in the storm. It's very precious.
Master takes comfort in it,
he is going to give it to Don Aranda's widow.
It's time for the pardon ceremony, Master.

[*Sound of clashing hatchets*]

DELANO

I am all for these hatchet-cleaners.
They are saving cargo. They make
an awful lot of pomp and racket though
about a few old, rusty knives.

BENITO

They think steel is worth its weight in gold.

[A slow solemn march is sounded on the gongs and other instruments. A gigantic coal-black NEGRO *comes up the steps. He wears a spiked iron collar to which a chain is attached that goes twice around his arms and ends padlocked to a broad band of iron. The* NEGRO *comes clanking forward and stands dumbly and like a dignitary in front of* BENITO. *Two small black boys bring* BENITO *a frail rattan cane and a silver ball, which they support on a velvet cushion.* BENITO *springs up, holds the ball, and raises the cane rigidly above the head of the negro in chains. For a moment, he shows no trace of sickness. The assembled blacks sing, "Evviva, Benito!" three times]*

BABU

[At one side with the Americans, but keeping an eye on BENITO]*

You are watching the humiliation of King Atufal,
once a ruler in Africa. He ruled as much land there
    as your President.
Poor Babu was a slave even in Africa,
a black man's slave, and now a white man's.

BENITO

[In a loud, firm voice]

Former King Atufal, I call on you to kneel!
Say, "My sins are black as night,
I ask the King of Spain's pardon
through his servant, Don Benito."

[Pause. ATUFAL *doesn't move]*

NEGROES

Your sins are black as night, King Atufal!
Your sins are black as night, King Atufal!

DELANO

What has King Atufal done?

BABU

I will tell you later, Yankee Captain.

BENITO

Ask pardon, former King Atufal.
If you will kneel,
I will strike away your chains.

[ATUFAL *slowly raises his chained arms and lets them drop*]

Ask pardon!

WOMAN SLAVE

Ask pardon King Atufal.

BENITO

Go!

[*Sound of instruments. The* BLACK BOYS *take* BENITO's *ball and cane. The straw chair is brought up.* BENITO *sits.* FRANCESCO *then leads him off-stage*]

BABU

Francesco!
I will be with you in a moment, Master.
You mustn't be afraid,
Francesco will serve you like a second Babu.

166

BENITO

Everyone serves me alike here,
but no one can serve me as you have.

BABU

I will be with you in a moment.
The Yankee master is at sea on our ship.
He wants me to explain our customs.

[BENITO *is carried off-stage*]

You would think Master's afraid of dying,
if Babu leaves him!

DELANO

I can imagine your tenderness during his sickness.
You were part of him,
you were almost a wife.

BABU

You say such beautiful things,
the United States must be a paradise for people like Babu.

DELANO

I don't know.
We have our faults. We have many states,
some of them could stand improvement.

BABU

The United States must be heaven.

DELANO

I suppose we have fewer faults than other countries.
What did King Atufal do?

BABU

He used the Spanish flag for toilet paper.

DELANO

That's treason.
Did Atufal know what he was doing?
Perhaps the flag was left somewhere it shouldn't have been.
Things aren't very strict here.

BABU

I never thought of that.
I will go and tell Master.

DELANO

Oh, no, you mustn't do that!
I never interfere with another man's ship.
Don Benito is your lord and dictator.
How long has this business with King Atufal been
    going on?

BABU

Ever since the yellow fever,
and twice a day.

DELANO

He did a terrible thing, but he looks like a royal fellow.
You shouldn't call him a king, though,
it puts ideas into his head.

BABU

Atufal had gold wedges in his ears in Africa;
how he wears a padlock and Master bears the key.

DELANO

I see you have a feeling for symbols of power.
You had better be going now,
Don Benito will be nervous about you.

[BABU *goes off*]

That was a terrible thing to do with a flag;
everything is untidy and unravelled here—
this sort of thing would never happen on the
    President Adams.

PERKINS

Your ship is as shipshape as our country, Sir.

DELANO

I wish people wouldn't take me as representative of
    our country:
America's one thing, I am another;
we shouldn't have to bear one another's burdens.

PERKINS

You are a true American for all your talk, Sir;
I can't believe you were mistaken for a Castilian Don.

DELANO

No one would take me for Don Benito.

PERKINS

I wonder if he isn't an imposter, some traveling actor from
    a circus?

DELANO

No, Cereno is a great name in Peru, like Winthrop or
    Adams with us.

I recognize the family features in our captain.

[*An* OLD SPANISH SAILOR, *grizzled and dirty, is seen crawling on all fours with an armful of knots toward the Americans. He points to where* BENITO *and* BABU *have disappeared and whistles. He holds up the knots as though he were in chains, then throws them out loosely on the deck in front of him. A* GROUP OF NEGROES *forms a circle around him, holding hands and singing childishly. Then, laughing, they carry the* SPANIARD *off-stage on their shoulders*]

These blacks are too familiar!
We are never alone!

[*Sound of gongs. Full minute's pause, as if time were passing.* DELANO *leans on the railing. The sun grows brighter*]

This ship is strange.
These people are too spontaneous—all noise and show,
no character!
Real life is a simple monotonous thing.
I wonder about that story about the calms;
it doesn't stick.
Don Benito hesitated himself in telling it.
No one could run a ship so stupidly,
and place three officers on one yard.

[BENITO *and* BABU *return*]

A captain has unpleasant duties;
I am sorry for you, Don Benito.

BENITO
You find my ship unenviable, Sir?

170

DELANO

I was talking about punishing Atufal;
he acted like an animal!

BENITO

Oh, yes, I was forgetting . . .
He was a King,
How long have you lain in at this island, Sir?

DELANO

Oh, a week today.

BENITO

What was your last port, Sir?

DELANO

Canton.

BENITO

You traded seal-skins and American muskets
for Chinese tea and silks, perhaps?

DELANO

We took in some silks.

BENITO

A little gold and silver too?

DELANO

Just a little silver. We are only merchants.
We take in a dollar here and there. We have no Peru,
or a Pizarro who can sweat gold out of the natives.

BENITO

You'll find things have changed

a little in Peru since Pizarro, Captain.

[*Starts to move away.* BABU *whispers to him, and he comes back abruptly, as if he had forgotten something important*]

How many men have you on board, Sir?

DELANO

Some twenty-five, Sir. Each man is at his post.

BENITO

They're all on board, Sir, now?

DELANO

They're all on board. Each man is working.

BENITO

They'll be on board tonight, Sir?

DELANO

Tonight? Why do you ask, Don Benito?

BENITO

Will they all be on board tonight, Captain?

DELANO

They'll be on board for all I know.

[PERKINS *makes a sign to* DELANO]

Well, no, to tell the truth, today's our Independence Day.
A gang is going ashore to see the village.
A little diversion improves their efficiency,
a little regulated corruption.

BENITO

You North Americans take no chances. Generally,
    I suppose,
even your merchant ships go more or less armed?

DELANO

A rack of muskets, sealing spears and cutlasses.
Oh, and a six-pounder or two; we are a sealing ship,
but with us each merchant is a privateer—
only in case of oppression, of course.
You've heard about how we shoot pirates.

BABU

Boom, boom, come Master.

> [BENITO *walks away on* BABU'S *arm and sits down, almost off-stage in his straw chair. They whisper. Meanwhile, a* SPANISH SAILOR *climbs the rigging furtively, spread-eagles his arms and shows a lace shirt under his shabby jacket. He points to* BENITO *and* BABU *and winks. At a cry from* ONE OF THE OAKUM PICKERS, THREE NEGROES *help the* SPANIARD *down with servile, ceremonious attentions*]

PERKINS

Did you see that sailor's lace shirt, Sir?
He must have robbed one of the cabin passengers.
I hear that people strip the dead
in these religious countries.

DELANO

No, you don't understand the Spaniards.
In these old Latin countries,
each man's a beggar or a noble, often both;
they have no middle class. With them it's customary

to sew a mess of gold and pearls on rags—
that's how an aristocracy that's going to the dogs
keeps up its nerve.

DELANO

It's odd though,
that Spanish sailor seemed to want to tell me something.
He ought to dress himself properly and speak his mind.
That's what we do. That's why we're strong:
everybody trusts us. Nothing gets done
when every man's a noble. I wonder why
the captain asked me all those questions?

PERKINS

He was passing the time of day, Sir;
It's a Latin idleness.

DELANO

It's strange. Did you notice how Benito stopped rambling?
He was conventional . . . consecutive for the first time
        since we met him.
Something's wrong. Perhaps, they've men below the decks,
a sleeping volcano of Spanish infantry. The Malays do it,
play sick and cut your throat.
A drifting boat, a dozen doped beggars on deck,
two hundred sweating murderers packed below
        like sardines—
that's rot! Anyone can see these people are really sick,
sicker than usual. Our countries are at peace.
I wonder why he asked me all those questions?

PERKINS

Just idle curiosity. I hear
the gentlemen of Lima sit at coffee-tables from sun to sun
and gossip. They don't even have women to look at;
they're all locked up with their aunts.

DELANO

Their sun is going down. These old empires go.
They are much too familiar with their blacks.
I envy them though, they have no character,
they feel no need to stand alone.
We stand alone too much,
that's why no one can touch us for sailing a ship;
When a country loses heart, it's easier to live.
Ah, Babu! I suppose Don Benito's indisposed again!
Tell him I want to talk to his people;
there's nothing like a well man to help the sick.

BABU

Master is taking his siesta, Yankee Master.
His siesta is sacred, I am afraid to disturb it.
Instead, let me show you our little entertainment.

DELANO

Let's have your entertainment;
if you know a man's pleasure
you know his measure.

BABU

We are a childish people. Our pleasures are childish.
No one helped us, we know nothing

about your important amusements,
such as killing seals and pirates.

DELANO

I'm game. Let's have your entertainment.

> [BABU *signals. The gong sounds ten times and the canvas is*
> *pulled from the circular structure. Enclosed in a triangular*
> *compartment, an* OLD SPANISH SAILOR *is dipping naked white*
> *dolls in a tar-pot*]

BABU

This little amusement keeps him alive, Yankee Master.
He is especially fond of cleaning the dolls
after he has dirtied them.

> [*The* OLD SPANISH SAILOR *laughs hysterically, and then smears*
> *his whole face with tar*]

OLD SPANISH SAILOR

My soul is white!

BABU

The yellow fever destroyed his mind.

DELANO

Let's move on. This man's brain,
as well as his face, is defiled with pitch!

BABU

He says his soul is white.

> [*The structure is pushed around and another triangular com-*
> *partment appears. A* NEGRO BOY *is playing chess against a*
> *splendid Spanish doll with a crown on its head. He stops and*
> *holds two empty wine bottles to his ears*]

This boy is deaf.
The yellow fever destroyed his mind.

DELANO

Why is he holding those bottles to his ears?

BABU

He is trying to be a rabbit,
or listening to the ocean, his mother—
who knows?

DELANO

If he's deaf, how can he hear the ocean?
Anyway, he can't hear me.
I pass, let's move on.

> [*The structure is pushed around to a third compartment. A* SPANISH SAILOR *is holding a big armful of rope*]

What are you knotting there, my man?

SPANISH SAILOR

The knot.

DELANO

So I see, but what's it for?

SPANISH SAILOR

For someone to untie. Catch!

> [*Throws the knot to* DELANO]

BABU

> [*Snatching the knot from* DELANO]

It's dirty, it will dirty your uniform.

177

DELANO

Let's move on. Your entertainment
is rather lacking in invention, Babu.

BABU

We have to do what we can
We are just beginners at acting.
This next one will be better.

> [*The structure is pushed around and shows a beautiful* NEGRO
> WOMAN. *She is dressed and posed as the Virgin Mary. A Christ-
> mas crèche is arranged around her. A* VERY WHITE SPANIARD
> *dressed as Saint Joseph stands behind her. She holds a Christ-
> child, the same crowned doll, only black, the* NEGRO BOY *was
> playing chess against*]

She is the Virgin Mary. That man is not the father.

DELANO

I see. I suppose her son is the King of Spain.

BABU

The Spaniards taught us everything,
there's nothing we can learn from you, Yankee Master.
When they took away our country, they gave us a
    better world.
Things do not happen in that world as they do here.

DELANO

That's a very beautiful,
though unusual Virgin Mary.

BABU

Yes, the Bible says, "I am black not white."
When Don Aranda was dying,

178

we wanted to give him the Queen of Heaven
because he took away our chains.

PERKINS

The Spaniards must have taught them everything;
they're all mixed up, they don't even know their religion.

DELANO

No, no! The Catholic Church doesn't just teach,
it knows how to take from its converts.

BABU

Do you want to shake hands with the Queen of Heaven,
    Yankee Master?

DELANO

No, I'm not used to royalty.
Tell her I believe in freedom of religion,
if people don't take liberties.
Let's move on.

BABU

    [*Kneeling to the Virgin Mary*]

I present something Your Majesty has never seen,
a white man who doesn't believe in taking liberties,
Your Majesty.

    [*The structure is pushed around and shows* ATUFAL *in chains
    but with a crown on his head*]

BABU

This is the life we believe in.

179

Ask pardon, King Atufal!
Kiss the Spanish flag!

DELANO

Please don't ask me to shake hands with King Atufal!

[*The canvas is put back on the structure*]

BABU

You look tired and serious, Yankee Master.
We have to have what fun we can.
We never would have lived through the deadly calms
without a little amusement.

[*Bows and goes off*]
[*The* NEGROES *gradually drift away.* DELANO *sighs with relief*]

DELANO

Well, that wasn't much!
I suppose Shakespeare started that way.

PERKINS

Who cares?
I see a speck on the blue sea, Sir,
our whaleboat is coming.

DELANO

A speck? My eyes are speckled.
I seem to have been dreaming. What's solid?

[*Touches the ornate railing; a piece falls onto the deck*]

This ship is nothing, Perkins!
I dreamed someone was trying to kill me!
How could he? Jack-of-the-beach,

they used to call me on the Duxbury shore.
Carrying a duck-satchel in my hand, I used to paddle
along the waterfront from a hulk to school.
I didn't learn much there. I was always shooting duck
or gathering huckleberries along the marsh with
    Cousin Nat!
I like nothing better than breaking myself on the surf.
I used to track the seagulls down the five-mile stretch
    of beach for eggs.
How can I be killed now at the ends of the earth
by this insane Spaniard?
Who could want to murder Amasa Delano?
My conscience is clean. God is good.
What am I doing on board this nigger-pirate ship?

PERKINS

You're not talking like a skipper, Sir.
Our boat's a larger spot now.

DELANO

I am childish.
I am doddering and drooling into my second childhood.
God help me, nothing's solid!

PERKINS

Don Benito, Sir. Touch him,
he's as solid as his ship.

DELANO

Don Benito? He's a walking ghost!

      [BENITO *comes up to* DELANO. BABU *is a few steps behind him*]

181

BENITO

I am the ghost of myself, Captain.
Excuse me, I heard you talking about dreams
        and childhood.
I was a child, too, once, I have dreams about it.

DELANO

        [*Starting*]

I'm sorry.
This jumping's just a nervous habit.
I thought you were part of my dreams.

BENITO

I was taking my siesta,
I dreamed I was a boy back in Lima.
I was with my brothers and sisters,
and we were dressed for the festival of Corpus Christi
like people at our Bourbon court.
We were simple children, but something went wrong;
little black men came on us with beetle backs.
They had caterpillar heads and munched away on our
        fine clothes.
They made us lick their horned and varnished insect legs.
Our faces turned brown from their spit,
we looked like bugs, but nothing could save our lives!

DELANO

Ha, ha, Captain. We are like two dreams meeting head-on.
My whaleboat's coming,
we'll both feel better over a bottle of cider.

[BABU *blows a bosun's whistle. The gongs are sounded with descending notes. The* NEGROES *assemble in ranks*]

BABU

It's twelve noon, Master Yankee.
Master wants his midday shave.

ALL THE NEGROES

Master wants his shave! Master wants his shave!

BENITO

Ah, yes, the razor! I have been talking too much.
You can see how badly I need a razor.
I must leave you, Captain.

BABU

No, Don Amasa wants to talk.
Come to the cabin, Don Amasa.
Don Amasa will talk, Master will listen.
Babu will lather and strop.

DELANO

I want to talk to you about navigation.
I am new to these waters.

BENITO

Doubtless, doubtless, Captain Delano.

PERKINS

I think I'll take my siesta, Sir.

[*He walks off*]
[BENITO, BABU, *and* DELANO *walk toward the back of the stage. A scrim curtain lifts, showing a light deck cabin that forms a sort of attic. The floor is matted, partitions that still leave*

splintered traces have been knocked out. To one side, a small table screwed to the floor; on it, a dirty missal; above it, a small crucifix, rusty crossed muskets on one side, rusty crossed cutlasses on the other. BENITO *sits down in a broken throne-like and gilded chair.* BABU *begins to lather. A magnificent array of razors, bottles and other shaving equipment lies on a table beside him. Behind him, a hammock with a pole in it and a dirty pillow*]

DELANO

So this is where you took your siesta.

BENITO

Yes, Captain, I rest here when my fate will let me.

DELANO

This seems like a sort of dormitory, sitting-room,
sail-loft, chapel, armory, and private bedroom all together.

BENITO

Yes, Captain: events have not been favorable
to much order in my personal arrangements.

[BABU *moves back and opens a locker. A lot of flags, torn shirts and socks tumble out. He takes one of the flags, shakes it with a flourish, and ties it around* BENITO's *neck*]

BABU

Master needs more protection.
I do everything I can to save his clothes.

DELANO

The Castle and the Lion of Spain.
Why, Don Benito, this is the flag of Spain you're using!
It's well it's only I and not the King of Spain who sees this!

All's one, though, I guess, in this carnival world.
I see you like gay colors as much as Babu.

BABU

   [*Giggling*]

The bright colors draw the yellow fever
from Master's mind.

   [*Raises the razor*]
   [BENITO *begins to shake*]

Now, Master, now, Master!

BENITO

You are talking while you hold the razor.

BABU

You mustn't shake so, Master.
Look, Don Amasa, Master always shakes when I shave him,
though he is braver than a lion and stronger than a castle.
Master knows Babu has never yet drawn blood.
I may, though, sometime, if he shakes so much.
Now, Master!
Come, Don Amasa, talk to Master about the gales
    and calms,
he'll answer and forget to shake.

DELANO

Those calms, the more I think of them the more I wonder.
You say you were two months sailing here;
I made that stretch in less than a week.
We never met with any calms.

If I'd not heard your story from your lips,
and seen your ruined ship,
I would have said something was missing,
I would have said this was a mystery ship.

BENITO

For some men the whole world is a mystery;
they cannot believe their senses.

[BENITO *shakes, the razor gets out of hand and cuts his cheek*]

Santa Maria!

BABU

Poor, poor Master, see, you shook so;
this is Babu's first blood.
Please answer Don Amasa, while I wipe
this ugly blood from the razor and strop it again.

BENITO

The sea was like the final calm of the world
On, on it went. It sat on us and drank our strength,
crosscurrents eased us out to sea,
the yellow fever changed our blood to poison.

BABU

You stood by us. Some of us stood by you!

BENITO

Yes, my Spanish crew was weak and surly, but the blacks,
the blacks were angels. Babu has kept me in this world.
I wonder what he is keeping me for?
You belong to me. I belong to you forever.

BABU

Ah, Master, spare yourself.
Forever is a very long time;
nothing's forever.

[*With great expertness, delicacy and gentleness,* BABU *massages* BENITO's *cheeks, shakes out the flag, pours lotion from five bottles on* BENITO's *hair, cleans the shaving materials, and stands off admiring his work*]

Master looks just like a statue.
He's like a figurehead, Don Amasa!

[DELANO *looks, then starts to walk out leaving* BENITO *and* BABU. *The curtain drops upon them.* DELANO *rejoins* PERKINS, *lounging at the rail*]

PERKINS

Our boat is coming.

DELANO

[*Gaily*]

I know!
I don't know how I'll explain this pomp
and squalor to my own comfortable family of a crew.
Even shaving here is like a High Mass.
There's something in a Negro, something
that makes him fit to have around your person.
His comb and brush are castanets.
What tact Babu had!
What noiseless, gliding briskness!

PERKINS

Our boat's about along side, Sir.

DELANO

What's more, the Negro has a sense of humor.
I don't mean their boorish giggling and teeth-showing,
I mean his easy cheerfulness in every glance and gesture.
You should have seen Babu toss that Spanish flag like
        a juggler,
and change it to a shaving napkin!

PERKINS

The boat's here, Sir.

DELANO

We need inferiors, Perkins,
more manners, more docility, no one has an inferior mind
        in America.

PERKINS

Here is your crew, Sir.

        [BABU *runs out from the cabin. His cheek is bleeding*]

DELANO

Why, Babu, what has happened?

BABU

Master will never get better from his sickness.
His bad nerves and evil fever made him use me so.
I gave him one small scratch by accident,
the only time I've nicked him, Don Amasa.
He cut me with his razor. Do you think I will die?
I'd rather die than bleed to death!

DELANO

It's just a pinprick, Babu. You'll live.

BABU

I must attend my master.

[*Runs back into cabin*]

DELANO

Just a pinprick, but I wouldn't have thought
Don Benito had the stuff to swing a razor.
Up north we use our fists instead of knives.
I hope Benito's not dodging around some old grindstone
in the hold, and sharpening a knife for me.
Here, Perkins, help our men up the ladder.

[*Two immaculate* AMERICAN SAILORS *appear carrying great
casks of water. Two more follow carrying net baskets of wilted
pumpkins. The* NEGROES *begin to crowd forward, shouting,
"We want Yankee food, we want Yankee drink!"* DELANO
grandiosely holds up a pumpkin; an OLD NEGRO *rushes forward, snatches at the pumpkin, and knocks* DELANO *off-balance
into* PERKINS'S *arms.* DELANO *gets up and knocks the* NEGRO
down with his fist. All is tense and quiet. The SIX HATCHET-
CLEANERS *lift their hatchets above their heads*]

DELANO

[*Furious*]

Americans, stand by me! Stand by your captain!

[*Like lightning, the* AMERICANS *unsling their muskets, fix bayonets, and kneel with their guns pointing at the* NEGROES]

Don Benito, Sir, call your men to order!

BABU

We're starving, Yankee Master. We mean no harm;
we've never been so scared.

DELANO

You try my patience, Babu.
I am talking to Captain Cereno;
call your men to order, Sir.

BENITO

Make them laugh, Babu. The Americans aren't going
to shoot.

[BABU *airily waves a hand. The* NEGROES *smile.* DELANO *turns
to* BENITO]

You mustn't blame them too much; they're sick
and hungry.
We have kept them cooped up for ages.

DELANO

[*As the* NEGROES *relax*]

Form them in lines, Perkins!
Each man shall have his share.
That's how we run things in the States—
to each man equally, no matter what his claims.

NEGROES

[*Standing back, bleating like sheep*]

Feed me, Master Yankee! Feed me, Master Yankee!

DELANO

You are much too close.
Here, Perkins, take the provisions aft.
You'll save lives by giving each as little as you can,
Be sure to keep a tally.

[FRANCESCO, *a majestic, yellow-colored mulatto, comes up to*
DELANO]

FRANCESCO

My master requests your presence at dinner, Don Amasa.

DELANO

Tell him I have indigestion.
Tell him to keep better order on his ship.
It's always the man of good will that gets hurt;
my fist still aches from hitting that old darky.

FRANCESCO

My master has his own methods of discipline
that are suitable for our unfortunate circumstances.
Will you come to dinner, Don Amasa?

DELANO

I'll come. When in Rome, do as the Romans.
Excuse my quick temper, Sir.
It's better to blow up than to smoulder.

[*The scrim curtain is raised. In the cabin, a long table loaded
with silver has been laid out. The locker has been closed and
the Spanish flag hangs on the wall.* DON BENITO *is seated,* BABU
stands behind him. As soon as DELANO *sits down,* FRANCESCO
begins serving with great dignity and agility]

FRANCESCO

A finger bowl, Don Amasa.

[*After each statement, he moves about the table*]

A napkin, Don Amasa.
A glass of American water, Don Amasa.

191

A slice of American pumpkin, Don Amasa.
A goblet of American cider, Don Amasa.

> [DELANO *drinks a great deal of cider,* BENITO *hardly touches his*]

DELANO

This is very courtly for a sick ship, Don Benito.
The Spanish Empire will never go down, if she keeps
      her chin up.

BENITO

I'm afraid I shan't live long enough to enjoy
      your prophecy.

DELANO

I propose a toast to the Spanish Empire
on which the sun never sets;
may you find her still standing, when you land, Sir!

BENITO

Our Empire has lasted three hundred years,
I suppose she will last another month.
I wish I could say the same for myself. My sun is setting,
I hear the voices of the dead in this calm.

DELANO

You hear the wind lifting;
it's bringing our two vessels together.
We are going to take you into port, Don Benito.

BENITO

You are either too late or too early with your good works.

Our yellow fever may break out again.
You aren't going to put your men in danger, Don Amasa?

DELANO

My boys are all healthy, sir.

BENITO

Health isn't God, I wouldn't trust it.

FRANCESCO

May I fill your glass, Don Amasa?

BABU

New wine in new bottles,
that's the American spirit, Yankee Master.
They say all men are created equal in North America.

DELANO

We prefer merit to birth, boy.

[BABU *motions imperiously for* FRANCESCO *to leave. As he goes,
bowing to the* CAPTAINS, FOUR NEGROES *play the* Marseillaise]

Why are they playing the *Marseillaise?*

BABU

His uncle is supposed to have been in the
French Convention,
and voted for the death of the French King.

DELANO

This polite and royal fellow is no anarchist!

BABU

Francesco is very *ancien regime,*
he is even frightened of the Americans.

He doesn't like the way you treated King George.
Babu is more liberal.

DELANO

A royal fellow,
this usher of yours, Don Benito!
He is as yellow as a goldenrod.
He is a king, a king of kind hearts.
What a pleasant voice he has!

BENITO

[*Glumly*]

Francesco is a good man.

DELANO

As long as you've known him,
he's been a worthy fellow, hasn't he?
Tell me, I am particularly curious to know.

BENITO

Francesco is a good man.

DELANO

I'm glad to hear it, I am glad to hear it!
You refute the saying of a planter friend of mine.
He said, "When a mulatto has a regular European face,
look out for him, he is a devil."

BENITO

I've heard your planter's remark applied
to intermixtures of Spaniards and Indians;
I know nothing about mulattoes.

194

DELANO

No, no, my friend's refuted;
if we're so proud of our white blood,
surely a little added to the blacks improves their breed.
I congratulate you on your servants, Sir.

BABU

We've heard that Jefferson, the King of your Republic,
would like to free his slaves.

DELANO

Jefferson has read too many books, boy,
but you can trust him. He's a gentleman and an American!
He's not lifting a finger to free his slaves.

BABU

We hear you have a new capital modelled on Paris,
and that your President is going to set up
a guillotine on the Capitol steps.

DELANO

Oh, Paris! I told you you could trust Mr. Jefferson, boy,
he stands for law and order like your mulatto.
Have you been to Paris, Don Benito?

BENITO

I'm afraid I'm just a provincial Spaniard, Captain.

DELANO

Let me tell you about Paris.
You know what French women are like—
nine parts sex and one part logic.
Well, one of them in Paris heard

that my ship was the *President Adams*. She said,
"You are descended from Adam, Captain,
you must know everything,
tell me how Adam and Eve learned to sleep together."
Do you know what I said?

BENITO

No, Captain.

DELANO

I said, "I guess Eve was a Frenchwoman,
the first Frenchwoman."
Do you know what she answered?

BENITO

No, Captain Delano.

DELANO

She said, "I was trying to provoke a philosophical
      discussion, Sir."
A philosophical discussion, ha, ha!
You look serious, Sir. You know, something troubles me.

BENITO

Something troubles you, Captain Delano?

DELANO

I still can't understand those calms,
but let that go. The scurvy,
why did it kill off three Spaniards in every four,
and only half the blacks?

Negroes are human, but surely you couldn't have
       favored them
before your own flesh and blood!

BENITO

This is like the Inquisition, Captain Delano.
I have done the best I could.

[BABU *dabs* BENITO's *forehead with cider*]

BABU

Poor, poor Master; since Don Aranda died,
he trusts no one except Babu.

DELANO

Your Babu is an uncommonly intelligent fellow;
you are right to trust him, Sir.
Sometimes I think we overdo our talk of freedom.
If you looked into our hearts, we all want slaves.

BENITO

Disease is a mysterious thing;
it takes one man, and leaves his friend.
Only the unfortunate can understand misfortune.

DELANO

I must return to my bosun;
he's pretty green to be left alone here.
Before I go I want to propose a last toast to you!
A good master deserves good servants!

[*He gets up. As he walks back to* PERKINS, *the scrim curtain
falls, concealing* BENITO *and* BABU]

That captain must have jaundice,
I wish he kept better order.
I don't like hitting menials.

PERKINS

I've done some looking around, Sir. I've used my eyes

DELANO

That's what they're for, I guess. You have to watch
     your step,
this hulk, this rotten piece of finery,
will fall apart. This old world needs new blood
and Yankee gunnery to hold it up.
You shouldn't mess around, though, it's their ship;
you're breaking all the laws of the sea.

PERKINS

Do you see that man-shaped thing in canvas?

DELANO

I see it.

PERKINS

Behind the cloth, there's a real skeleton,
a man dressed up like Don Benito.

DELANO

They're Catholics, and worship bones.

PERKINS

There's writing on its coat. It says,
"I am Don Aranda," and, "Follow your leader."

198

DELANO

Follow your leader?

PERKINS

I saw two blacks unfurling a flag,
a black skull and crossbones on white silk.

DELANO

That's piracy. We've been ordered
to sink any ship that flies that flag.
Perhaps they were playing.

PERKINS

I saw King Atufal throw away his chains,
He called for food, the Spaniards served him two pieces
    of pumpkin,
and a whole bottle of your cider.

DELANO

Don Benito has the only key to Atufal's padlock.
My cider was for the captain's table.

PERKINS

Atufal pointed to the cabin where you were dining,
and drew a finger across his throat.

DELANO

Who could want to kill Amasa Delano?

PERKINS

I warned our men to be ready for an emergency.

DELANO

You're a mind reader,

I couldn't have said better myself;
but we're at peace with Spain.

PERKINS

I told them to return with loaded muskets
and fixed bayonets.

DELANO

Here comes Benito. Watch how I'll humor him
and sound him out.

[BABU *brings out* BENITO'S *chair.* BENITO *sits in it*]

It's good to have you back on deck, Captain.
Feel the breeze! It holds and will increase.
My ship is moving nearer. Soon we will be together.
We have seen you through your troubles.

BENITO

Remember, I warned you about the yellow fever.
I am surprised you haven't felt afraid.

DELANO

Oh, that will blow away.
Everything is going to go better and better;
the wind's increasing, soon you'll have no cares.
After the long voyage, the anchor drops into the harbor.
It's a great weight lifted from the captain's heart.
We are getting to be friends, Don Benito.
My ship's in sight, the *President Adams!*
How the wind braces a man up!
I have a small invitation to issue to you.

BENITO

An invitation?

DELANO

I want you to take a cup of coffee
with me on my quarter deck tonight.
The Sultan of Turkey never tasted such coffee
as my old steward makes. What do you say, Don Benito?

BENITO

I cannot leave my ship.

DELANO

Come, come, you need a change of climate.
The sky is suddenly blue, Sir,
my coffee will make a man of you.

BENITO

I cannot leave my ship.
Even now, I don't think you understand my position here.

DELANO

I want to speak to you alone.

BENITO

I am alone, as much as I ever am.

DELANO

In America, we don't talk about money
in front of servants and children.

BENITO

Babu is not my servant.
You spoke of money—since the yellow fever,

he has had a better head for figures than I have.

DELANO

You embarrass me, Captain,
but since circumstances are rather special here,
I will proceed.

BENITO

Babu takes an interest in all our expenses.

DELANO

Yes, I am going to talk to you about your expenses.
I am responsible to my owners for all
the sails, ropes, food and carpentry I give you.
You will need a complete rerigging, almost a new ship,
    in fact,
You shall have our services at cost.

BENITO

I know, you are a merchant.
I suppose I ought to pay you for our lives.

DELANO

I envy you, Captain. You are the only owner
of the *San Domingo,* since Don Aranda died.
I am just an employee. Our owners would sack me,
if I followed my better instincts.

BENITO

You can give your figures to Babu, Captain.

DELANO

You are very offhand about money, Sir;

I don't think you realize the damage that has been done
    to your ship.
Ah, you smile. I'm glad you're loosening up.
Look, the water gurgles merrily, the wind is high,
a mild light is shining. I sometimes think
such a tropical light as this must have shone
on the tents of Abraham and Isaac.
It seems as if Providence were watching over us.

PERKINS

There are things that need explaining here, Sir.

DELANO

Yes, Captain, Perkins saw some of your men
unfurling an unlawful flag,
a black skull and crossbones.

BENITO

You know my only flag is the Lion and Castle of Spain.

DELANO

No, Perkins says he saw a skull and crossbones.
That's piracy. I trust Perkins.
You've heard about how my government blew
the bowels out of the pirates at Tripoli?

BENITO

Perhaps my Negroes . . .

DELANO

My government doesn't intend
to let you play at piracy!

BENITO

Perhaps my Negroes were playing.
When you take away their chains . . .

DELANO

I'll see that you are all put back in chains,
if you start playing pirates!

PERKINS

There's something else he can explain, Sir.

DELANO

Yes, Perkins saw Atufal throw off his chains
and order dinner.

BABU

Master has the key, Yankee Master.

BENITO

I have the key.
You can't imagine how my position exhausts me, Captain.

DELANO

I can imagine. Atufal's chains are fakes.
You and he are in cahoots, Sir!

PERKINS

They don't intend to pay for our sails and service.
They think America is Santa Claus.

DELANO

The United States are death on pirates and debtors.

PERKINS

There's one more thing for him to explain, Sir.

DELANO

Do you see that man-shaped thing covered with black
   cloth, Don Benito?

BENITO

I always see it.

DELANO

Take away the cloth. I order you to take away the cloth!

BENITO

I cannot. Oh, Santa Maria, have mercy!

DELANO

Of course, you can't. It's no Virgin Mary.
You have done something terrible to your friend,
   Don Aranda.
Take away the cloth, Perkins!

   [*As* PERKINS *moves forward,* ATUFAL *suddenly stands chainless
   and with folded arms, blocking his way*]

BABU

   [*Dancing up and down and beside himself*]

Let them see it! Let them see it!
I can't stand any more of their insolence;
the Americans treat us like their slaves!

   [BABU *and* PERKINS *meet at the man-shaped object and start
   pulling away the cloth.* BENITO *rushes between them, and
   throws them back and sprawling on the deck.* BABU *and* PER-
   KINS *rise, and stand hunched like wrestlers, about to close in
   on* BENITO, *who draws his sword with a great gesture. It is only
   a hilt. He runs at* BABU *and knocks him down.* ATUFAL *throws*

off his chains and signals to the HATCHET-CLEANERS. *They stand behind* BENITO *with raised hatchets. The* NEGROES *shout ironically,* "Evviva Benito!"]

You too, Yankee Captain!
If you shoot, we'll kill you.

DELANO

If a single American life is lost,
I will send this ship to the bottom,
and all Peru after it.
Do you hear me, Don Benito?

BENITO

Don't you understand? I am as powerless as you are!

BABU

He is as powerless as you are.

BENITO

Don't you understand? He has been holding a knife at
    my back.
I have been talking all day to save your life.

BABU

   [*Holding a whip*]

Do you see this whip? When Don Aranda was out
    of temper,
he used to snap pieces of flesh off us with it.
Now I hold the whip.
When I snap it, Don Benito jumps!

   [*Snaps the whip.* DON BENITO *flinches*]

206

DELANO

[*Beginning to understand*]

It's easy to terrorize the defenseless.

BABU

That's what we thought when Don Aranda held the whip.

DELANO

You'll find I am made of tougher stuff than your Spaniards.

ATUFAL

We want to kill you.

NEGROES

We want to kill you, Yankee Captain.

DELANO

Who could want to kill Amasa Delano?

BABU

Of course. We want to keep you alive.
We want you to sail us back to Africa.
Has anyone told you how much you are worth, Captain?

DELANO

I have another course in mind.

BABU

Yes, there's another course if you don't like Africa, there's
    another course.
King Atufal, show the Yankee captain
the crew that took the other course!

[*Three dead* SPANISH SAILORS *are brought on stage*]

ATUFAL

Look at Don Aranda?

BABU

Yes, you are hot-tempered and discourteous, Captain.
I am going to introduce you to Don Aranda.
You have a new command, Captain. You must meet your
    new owner.

[*The black cloth is taken from the man-shaped object and
shows a chalk-white skeleton dressed like* DON BENITO]

Don Amasa, Don Aranda!
You can see that Don Aranda was a white man like you,
because his bones are white.

NEGROES

He is a white because his bones are white!
He is a white because his bones are white!

ATUFAL

[*Pointing to the ribbon on the skeleton's chest*]

Do you see that ribbon?
It says, "Follow the leader."
We wrote it in his blood.

BABU

He was a white man
even though his blood was red as ours.

NEGROES

He is white because his bones are white!

BABU

Don Aranda is our figurehead,
we are going to chain him to the bow of our ship
to scare off devils.

ATUFAL

This is the day of Jubilee,
I am raising the flag of freedom!

NEGROES

Freedom! Freedom! Freedom!

> [*The black skull and crossbones is raised on two poles. The*
> NEGROES *form two lines, leading up to the flag, and leave an*
> *aisle. Each man is armed with some sort of weapon*]

BABU

Spread out the Spanish flag!

> [*The Lion and Castle of Spain is spread out on the deck in*
> *front of the skull and crossbones*]

The Spanish flag is the road to freedom.
Don Benito mustn't hurt his white feet on the splinters.

> [*Kneeling in front of* BENITO]

Your foot, Master!

> [BENITO *holds out his foot.* BABU *takes off* BENITO's *shoes*]

Give Don Benito back his sword!

> [*The sword-hilt is fastened back in* BENITO's *scabbard*]

Load him with chains!

> [*Two heavy chains are draped on* BENITO's *neck. The cane*
> *and ball are handed to him*]

Former Captain Benito Cereno, kneel!
Ask pardon of man!

BENITO

> [*Kneeling*]

I ask pardon for having been born a Spaniard.
I ask pardon for having enslaved my fellow man.

BABU

Strike off the oppressor's chain!

> [*One of* BENITO's *chains is knocked off, then handed to* ATU-
> FAL, *who dashes it to the deck*]

Former Captain Benito Cereno,
you must kiss the flag of freedom.

> [*Points to* DON ARANDA]

Kiss the mouth of the skull!

> [BENITO *walks barefoot over the Spanish flag and kisses the
> mouth of* DON ARANDA]

NEGROES

Evviva Benito! Evviva Benito!

> [*Sounds are heard from* PERKINS, *whose head has been covered
> with the sack*]

ATUFAL

The bosun wants to kiss the mouth of freedom.

BABU

March over the Spanish flag, Bosun.

> [PERKINS *starts forward*]

DELANO

You are dishonoring your nation, Perkins!
Don't you stand for anything?

PERKINS

I only have one life, Sir.

[*Walks over the Spanish flag and kisses the mouth of the skull*]

NEGROES

Evviva Bosun! *Evviva* Bosun!

DELANO

You are no longer an American, Perkins!

BABU

He was free to choose freedom, Captain.

ATUFAL

Captain Delano wants to kiss the mouth of freedom.

BABU

He is jealous of the bosun.

ATUFAL

In the United States, all men are created equal.

BABU

Don't you want to kiss the mouth of freedom, Captain?

DELANO

[*Lifting his pocket and pointing the pistol*]

Do you see what I have in my hand?

BABU

A pistol.

DELANO

I am unable to miss at this distance.

BABU

You must take your time, Yankee Master.
You must take your time.

DELANO

I am unable to miss.

BABU

You can stand there like a block of wood
as long as you want to, Yankee Master.
You will drop asleep, then we will tie you up,
and make you sail us back to Africa.

[*General laughter. Suddenly, there's a roar of gunfire. Several*
NEGROES, *mostly women, fall.* AMERICAN SEAMAN *in spotless
blue and white throw themselves in a lying position on deck.*
MORE *kneel above them, then* MORE *stand above these. All
have muskets and fixed bayonets. The First Row fires. More*
NEGROES *fall. They start to retreat. The Second Row fires.
More* NEGROES *fall. They retreat further. The Third Row fires.
The Three* AMERICAN LINES *march forward, but all the* NE-
GROES *are either dead or in retreat.* DON BENITO *has been
wounded. He staggers over to* DELANO *and shakes his hand*]

BENITO

You have saved my life.
I thank you for my life.

212

DELANO

A man can only do what he can,
We have saved American lives.

PERKINS

[*Pointing to* ATUFAL's *body*]

We have killed King Atufal,
we have killed their ringleader.

[BABU *jumps up. He is unwounded*]

BABU

I was the King. Babu, not Atufal
was the king, who planned, dared and carried out
the seizure of this ship, the *San Domingo*.
Untouched by blood myself, I had all
the most dangerous and useless Spaniards killed.
I freed my people from their Egyptian bondage.
The heartless Spaniards slaved for me like slaves.

[BABU *steps back, and quickly picks up a crown from the litter*]

This is my crown.

[*Puts crown on his head. He snatches* BENITO's *rattan cane*]

This is my rod.

[*Picks up silver ball*]

This is the earth.

[*Holds the ball out with one hand and raises the cane*]

This is the arm of the angry God.

[*Smashes the ball*]

PERKINS

Let him surrender. Let him surrender.
We want to save someone.

BENITO

My God how little these people understand!

BABU

[*Holding a white handkerchief and raising both his hands*]

Yankee Master understand me. The future is with us.

DELANO

[*Raising his pistol*]

This is your future.

[BABU *falls and lies still.* DELANO *pauses, then slowly empties the five remaining barrels of his pistol into the body. Lights dim*]

CURTAIN

Introduction (1965)

Benito Cereno is the third play in the extraordinary theater trilogy by Robert Lowell called *The Old Glory,* a work in which the renowned poet has fashioned a dramatic history of the American character. Held together by the unifying symbol of the flag, *The Old Glory* is based on stories by Hawthorne and a novella by Melville, but while Mr. Lowell has managed to adapt these tales with relative fidelity to the original texts, he has made them wholly and uniquely his own work. Invested with the author's keen historical sense and marvelous gift for language, the source materials assume the thickness and authority of myth; ritual and metaphors abound; traditional literature and historical events begin to function like Greek mythology, as the source and reflection of contemporary behavior. Mr. Lowell feels the past working in his very bones. And it is his subtle achievement not only to have evoked this past, but also to have superimposed the present upon it, so that the plays manage to look forward and backward at the same time. Adopting a style which is purposely chilling, measured and remote, he has endowed his plays with flinty intelligence and tautened passion, making them work on the spectator with all the suggestive power of non-discursive poems.

The three plays examine the American character at three different points in its historical development. This character the author finds to be permeated with violence from its beginnings—a violence which invariably erupts out in moments of panic. In *Endecott and the Red Cross,* a mild-mannered Puritan military man, faced with high-living Anglican-Royalists in colonial America, is forced into shedding blood by political-religious expediency; and in *My Kinsman, Major Molineux,* the American Revolution unfolds as a violent nightmare experienced by two Deerfield youths seeking out their British cousin in Boston, "the city of the dead."

In *Benito Cereno,* the third and finest play, Mr. Lowell brings us to the beginning of the 19th century and proceeds to unearth the seeds of our current discords. Based on Herman Melville's novella of the same name, *Benito Cereno* has all the theatrical power of the first two plays, as well as a heavily charged prose style and a strong suspenseful narrative. Melville's story is largely concerned with the shadow cast over a civilized mind by the primitive darkness. Mr. Lowell heightens this theme, examining along the way the ambiguous American attitude towards slavery and servitude.

In the American Place Theatre production, Jonathan Miller, the director, paced this play with an eye to its half-languorous, half-ominous atmosphere, giving it the rhythm of "an ocean undulating in long scoops of swells," but finally letting it explode into a shocking climax, to the accompaniment of discharging muskets. The visual effects of the original production, with its simple set and illustrative costuming, were excellent (the crisp uniforms of the American officers in black cutaway coats and white tights juxtaposed against the shabby-sumptuous attire of Cereno and the rags of the slaves). But it is the acting that was really unusual. In an age of flaccid, self-indulgent histrionics, Mr. Miller evoked performances of extraordinary depth, control and energy. Three actors in particular were superb: Roscoe Lee Browne, alternating between Calypso sunniness and sinister threat as Babu; Lester Rawlins, suave, smug and self-satisfied as Delano; and Frank Langella as Cereno, his eyes continually lowered with shame, his voice morose and rich, a trembling wreck of stateliness and nobility. But it is a violation to single out individuals for praise when the entire cast was functioning with that precision and power that we have come to expect only from long-established repertory companies.

The Old Glory, certainly, is the first American play to utilize historical materials in a compelling theatrical manner (just compare it with those lifeless high-school pageants that Maxwell Anderson used to grind out), perhaps because it is the first such play to assume a mature intellect on the part of its audience. After years of prosaic language, mundane forms and retarded themes—obstacles which only O'Neill was able to transcend successfully in his last plays, and then only through sheer doggedness and will—the American drama has finally developed an important subject and an eloquent voice. *The Old Glory* may well mark the beginning of a dramatic renaissance in America, during which our theater—like our fiction and poetry—will be able to tap the sources of our inmost being, and not just sink us deeper into narcosis and complacency. *Benito Cereno* is a cultural-poetic masterpiece, but the entire trilogy is an event of great moment. For it heralds the arrival not just of a brilliant new dramatist but of one who may very well come to revolutionize the American theater.

ROBERT BRUSTEIN

Director's note (1965)

I think it was John Locke, the English philosopher, who defined property as that with which a man hath mixed his labor. By that token, in directing Robert Lowell's *The Old Glory*, I feel that I have a small stake in the United States of America.

When I last came to America, I came with an English show, *Beyond the Fringe*, grafted a piece of my own country onto the fat carcass of Broadway and did very nicely thank you. But there was no mixture with America in it at all, and while I enjoyed the experience I always felt that I was on the outside looking in. *The Old Glory* changed all that, however. For the first time I was able to work with a great American writer and also had the chance of mixing my labor with nearly one hundred American theatrical workmen.

The play was mounted in an unusual way. It was a great poet's first entry into the theater and at the same time we were in on the start of a new dramatic experiment, which actually involved building the premises while we were rehearsing. It was the most extraordinary example of mass cooperation that I have ever known. During the nine weeks of casting and rehearsals I kept searching for a satisfactory metaphor to describe all this and I finally saw it in terms of *Treasure Island*.

Lowell was like Jim Hawkins, who had inherited a strange treasure map. His text was full of exotic instructions and rich proposals, all pointing the way to some unprecedented reward of new drama. With this chart in my hands I signed on the crew of actors, musicians and designers while the keel of our *Hispaniola* was being laid in the nave of St. Clement's Church. The whole adventure came as a delicious shock which unfolded more and more unexpected pleasures as the weeks went by. For I had been warned before coming back to the States that American actors were incapable of playing with the necessary formal high style which Lowell's text demanded, and that no American cast could subordinate its egotism to the stringent requirements of meticulous ensemble playing.

I had been told also that Americans were incapable of beautiful diction. This was especially alarming in *Benito Cereno,* since Lowell had written long swells of superb verse which called for an almost operatic vocal mastery. Once again, my fears proved groundless. Lester Rawlins, Frank Langella, and Roscoe Lee Browne rose magnificently to the occasion and startled even the author with the rich, complex possibilities of his own writing. Along with Jack Ryland the four worked together like a string quartet that had rehearsed in collaboration for years. There was also the cast of Negro extras who worked together with a fierce conscientiousness which I had never seen before on the American stage.

Looking back in pleasure over all this, I can only repeat what I must have said over and over again to the cast of these two plays. That is was an honor and a privilege to work with such noble and talented people.

Director's Note

These are difficult plays to mount and I only arrived at what seemed to me to be an entirely satisfactory solution with the last two pieces in the trilogy. The first play presents the most awkward puzzles for a director who has to marry scenes of ritual festivity with long passages of contemplative recitative. The essence of "Endecott and the Red Cross" seems to me to be its complex spiritual irony, and this can be easily swamped by the spectacle of the mid-summer fête. In the first production we never entirely got over this problem and after a lot of rehearsal, cutting and re-writing, we had to drop the play before the first night which seriously damaged the grand design. But it is possible that this play needs to be expanded anyway and presented as a full length piece on its own.

My Kinsman, Major Molineux is the most stylized of the three plays and it needs to be put across with scintillating artificiality. The costume designer, Willa Kim, and I worked on the basic idea of the 18th century political cartoon which dramatized the violent fervour of the times and gave it an almost surrealist nightmare sting. We painted the actors chalk grey and dressed them in costumes made of stiff unbleached cotton. The pockets and embroidery were drawn on in black ink so that the cast looked like pieces of paper cut out of a coffee-house broadsheet. Everyone except Robin and his brother was then very strictly choreographed so that they came and went like crude putty coloured marionettes. The controlling image for all this was Alice-in-Wonderland—as if the flesh and blood Deerfield boys had wandered into a dream world of sloganeering playing cards. When Molineux is struck down at the end his crude features should suddenly and shockingly leak scarlet blood. Somewhere in the revolutionary crowd I put a corpse in a winding sheet as if the hot wind of revolution had wakened the dead. Gilray and Lewis Carroll are the figures to keep in mind here.

I was driven by two ideas for *Benito Cereno,* the last play. First, as regards staging and diction, it seemed to me that Lowell had written an opera without music and the four principal actors were directed to move and speak as if they were soloists in an oratorio and they should be placed on the stage as if they were delivering Mozartian quartets and duets—very formal with no restless modern naturalism. This play seemed to me to be like a new *Tempest* with the Spanish captain playing a sort of drugged Prospero held captive by his Negro Babu. This idea turns the Spanish boat into a black magic island where all the normal laws of nature and society are relaxed and paralysed. The vision of the American captain is blurred by the heat, the lethargy and the exotic languor of the Negro slaves. Everything in this production must be bent towards creating this sense of lethargy. The Negroes need only to be seen on stage in ones and twos, mending nets and so on, unless otherwise indicated. Then from time to time they should all hum on one note in unison so as to create a vague off stage murmur like hives on a summer day. The entertainment should be baroque and courtly with no concession made to modern nightclub negritude. By the end of it, Delano should be sent off into a trance of drowsy reminiscence, as if Odysseus had succumbed after all in the palace of Circe. When final violence comes it should puncture the poisoned atmosphere which ought to have been slowly and lingeringly inflated throughout the evening. Finally, when everything

Director's Note

is still on the deck, Babu dead, and Delano upright amongst
the bloody debris, a Negro girl should come on stage slowly,
pause and give a long, awkward ghastly scream—like a
wounded albatross.

JONATHAN MILLER

The Old Glory, as produced at The American Place Theatre, was the winner of five Obie Awards for the 1964-65 season, including Best Play.